"It's taken me far too long to see the Bible as God's story. Elisabeta Karp is a writer and teacher who helps me see how God has woven both the Old and New Testaments together, pointing us all toward Messiah Jesus... Elisabeta takes us on a profound journey of messianic prophecy, showing us how all of the Bible is purposeful, intentional, and woven together as God's grand story."

—ESTHER FLEECE ALLEN
Author of *No More Faking Fine: Ending the Pretending*

"The Bible is many things, one being Israel's family diary. Having long advocated for looking at Scripture with a narrative lens—a typically Jewish approach—I was immediately struck by Elisabeta Karp's presentation. She brings a creative hermeneutical approach to biblical interpretation in her easy-to-read book. Those wishing to better grasp God's word and connect the dots between the Old and New Testaments will find her work very helpful. Happy to commend."

—JEFFREY SEIF
Executive Director, Union of Messianic Jewish Congregations

"In the pass of Cirith Ungol, the wise hobbit Sam turns to his friend Frodo and reflects, 'I wonder what sort of tale we've fallen into?' The question instantly clears the fog and reminds us, with shocking clarity, that each of us finds ourself in a story far more profound and magnificent than our own. It is within this heart-pounding premise that Elisabeta Karp shows us not only the Bible's grand story, but the countless ripples that resonate throughout. Having studied the Bible for nearly fifty years, I was shocked and delighted by all that I learned from *The Story Ripples of the Bible*. May you be similarly captivated, and may the ripple effect of your own devotion spill into the lives of all whom you encounter!"

—SCOTT BROWN
Missionary, Chosen People Ministries

"In our late modern era, people are looking for more than left-brain analytical, abstract thinking. They want more than lectures, outlines and bullet points. They are hungry for stories. The genius of the Bible is that it is the grand and true story of the world. Long after all the dissertations have been written, defended, and collected dust on shelves, these stories will continue to resound, reverberate, and ripple to the end of time. With her master metaphor of 'story ripples,' Elisabeta Karp has illuminated for us the inspired dynamic of Scripture, and the supernatural providence of God in 'HisStory.' The Creator drops these stones—of the archetypal stories of real events recorded in the Hebrew Bible—into the deep waters of history. And when their waves and ripples hit you and me, we are immersed in the same primordial flow of living water that was God's relational activity with his earliest people. Karp helps us understand how the mother of all Bible studies on the road to Emmaus must have transpired (Luke 24:27). How did Jesus explain how Moses wrote of him? Surely messianic prophecy is not merely stated predictions in propositional form but also embedded in the stories of the Torah and the Hebrew Bible, as they pre-figure the Messiah. The church will not be successful in fulfilling her mandate to win the Jewish people to Messiah (Rom 11:11–14) by philosophical apologetics or systematic theological discourse. She will need to re-tell their stories showing how they inherently point to Messiah Jesus. With fresh language and insights into the deep patterns of story, Karp's work demonstrates the unity of the Bible as one book, with waves going in one direction, toward the Messiah and the consummation of his kingdom. Whether we are communicating with younger late-modern Westerners, the majority non-Western world, or the Jewish people, we need the biblical communication dynamics of Karp's *The Story Ripples of the Bible*."

—WILLIAM BJORAKER
Co-author with Tom Steffen of *The Return of Oral Hermeneutics: As Good Today as It Was for the Hebrew Bible and First-Century Christianity*

The Story Ripples
of the Bible

The Story Ripples of the Bible

How Stories in Scripture Move Toward Messiah

by
ELISABETA KARP

Foreword by Zhava Glaser

WIPF & STOCK · Eugene, Oregon

THE STORY RIPPLES OF THE BIBLE
How Stories in Scripture Move Toward Messiah

Copyright © 2025 Elisabeta Karp. All rights reserved. Except for brief quotations in critical publications or reviews, no part of this book may be reproduced in any manner without prior written permission from the publisher. Write: Permissions, Wipf and Stock Publishers, 199 W. 8th Ave., Suite 3, Eugene, OR 97401.

Wipf & Stock
An Imprint of Wipf and Stock Publishers
199 W. 8th Ave., Suite 3
Eugene, OR 97401

www.wipfandstock.com

PAPERBACK ISBN: 979-8-3852-2235-3
HARDCOVER ISBN: 979-8-3852-2236-0
EBOOK ISBN: 979-8-3852-2237-7

VERSION NUMBER 082525

While I relish the enlightening world of seminary, this book is dedicated to all who desire to deepen their study of the Bible and grasp key connections between the Old and New Testaments without the hurdles of theological jargon.

Therefore every scribe who has been trained for the kingdom of heaven is like a master of a house, who brings out of his treasure what is new and what is old."
—Matthew 13:52

Contents

Permissions | ix
Foreword by Zhava Glaser | xi

Introduction | 1

Chapter Abraham | 17
    Story Ripple: Disinheritance and Regrafting | 17
    Story Ripple: From Barren to Bearing | 26

Chapter Joseph | 32
    Story Ripple: The Good News of Reconciliation | 32

Chapter Moses | 37
    Moses and Messiah Parallels | 37
    Theme: Unique Relationship and Appearance | 41
    Story Ripple: A Key Gentile Encounter | 46
    Story Ripple: Building a Dwelling Place for God | 52
    Story Ripple: Redemption Rises in the East | 59
    The Exodus (Ripple) Effect: From Israel's Deliverance to Your Redemption | 66

Chapter Israel | 72
    Story Ripple: The Hope of a New Covenant | 72
    Jesus' Desert Testing Parallels Israel's Wilderness Wandering | 77

Chapter David | 91
    PART ONE
        Messianic Beginnings: Parallels between Samuel and John the Baptist | 92
        Re-reading David and Goliath as Messianic Prophecy | 93
    PART TWO
    Isaiah's Suffering Servant: A Joseph-Like David | 106

PART THREE
    New Testament Theology | 113
    Three Ancient Promises | 118

Chapter Esther | 126
    Divine Favor in the Book of Esther | 127
    Messianic Parallels: Esther and Jesus | 128
    The Genius of Irony in the Book of Esther | 132

Conclusion | 138

Bibliography | 143

Permissions

© 2021 Jord A Lil Music (BMI) / Be Essential Songs (BMI) / Aaron Moses Chiriboga Music (BMI) / Holmeboy Music Group (BMI) / Jesse L. Cline Publishing Designee (BMI) (admin at EssentialMusicPublishing.com). All Rights Reserved. Used by Permission.

Title: I Thank God
Writers: Aaron Moses Chiriboga, Chuck Butler, Enrique Holmes, Maryanne George, Dante Bowe, Jesse Cline
Controlled Label Copy: © 2020 Heritage Worship Music Publishing (BMI) / Maverick City Publishing (BMI) (admin by Heritage Worship Music Publishing) / MJ George Music (BMI) (admin by Heritage Worship Music Publishing) / Bethel Worship Publishing (BMI). All Rights Reserved. Used by Permission. Bethel Music Total Control: 33.33%

Title: No Longer Slaves
Writers: Jonathan Helser, Brian Johnson, Joel Case
Controlled Label Copy: © 2014 Bethel Music Publishing (ASCAP). All Rights Reserved. Used by Permission. Bethel Music Total Control: 100%

Unless otherwise indicated, all Scripture quotations are from the ESV® Bible (The Holy Bible, English Standard Version®), © 2001 by Crossway, a publishing ministry of Good News Publishers. Used by permission. All rights reserved. The ESV text may not be quoted in any publication made available to the public by a Creative Commons license. The ESV may not be translated in whole or in part into any other language.

Scripture quotations marked NIV are taken from the Holy Bible, New International Version®, NIV®. Copyright © 1973, 1978, 1984, 2011 by Biblica, Inc.™ Used by permission of Zondervan. All rights reserved worldwide. www.zondervan.com The "NIV" and "New International Version" are trademarks registered in the United States Patent and Trademark Office by Biblica, Inc.™

Scripture quotations marked HCSB are taken from the Holman Christian Standard Bible®, Copyright © 1999, 2000, 2002, 2003, 2009 by Holman Bible Publishers. Used

PERMISSIONS

by permission. Holman Christian Standard Bible®, Holman CSB®, and HCSB® are federally registered trademarks of Holman Bible Publishers.

Scripture quotations marked NASB or NASB95 are taken from the (NASB®) New American Standard Bible®, Copyright © 1960, 1971, 1977, 1995, 2020 by The Lockman Foundation. Used by permission. All rights reserved. lockman.org

Scripture quotations marked NRSVUE are taken from the New Revised Standard Version Updated Edition. Copyright © 2021 National Council of Churches of Christ in the United States of America. Used by permission. All rights reserved worldwide.

Foreword

THE BIBLE IS NOT just a collection of doctrines, laws, prophecies, and wise sayings. At its heart, the Bible is a story—the grand story of God's unfolding plan to redeem a people for himself. And like any great epic, the biblical narrative is woven with key themes, patterns, and "ripples" that build and develop until they crescendo in a stunning climax—the person and work of Jesus the Messiah.

In this insightful book, Elisabeta Karp recovers a profoundly Jewish and biblical way of reading the Hebrew Scriptures. With her concept of "story ripples," Karp shows how the major stories, events, and figures of the Old Testament function as prophetic foreshadowings that find their ultimate fulfillment in the Messiah. She demonstrates how biblical prophecy is so much more than isolated predictions but is embedded in the very fabric of the scriptural narrative.

By tracing key messianic story ripples from the Torah, Prophets, and Writings, Karp opens our eyes afresh to the profound unity between the Old and New Testaments. She recaptures how deeply rooted Jesus and the New Testament gospel are in the bedrock of Israel's story. In the process, she recovers the centrality of Israel in God's cosmic drama of redemption.

As you read this book, don't be surprised if your mind is stretched, your heart starts to burn within you, and you begin to recognize Jesus anew in the Hebrew Bible. Karp's insights will fuel your love for the Scriptures as a unified witness to the Messiah and will enrich your ability to see and savor him in all of God's word.

This book is neither a heavy theological treatise nor fluffy inspirational fare. Mixing academic research with thoughtful reflection, *The Story Ripples of the Bible* is an eye-opening and thrilling journey through the Bible with Jesus himself as your tour guide, opening up the Scriptures to show how they all point to him. So settle in, and prepare to encounter the

Foreword

Messiah in the pages of Moses and the Prophets as never before. I trust this book will be a tool the Spirit uses to make the written word come alive with new clarity, coherence, and wonder as it reveals the beauty of the Living Word, Jesus.

Zhava Glaser, PhD
Associate Professor, Feinberg Center for Messianic Jewish Studies
Talbot School of Theology, Biola University

Introduction

IF YOU COULD TIME TRAVEL to anywhere in the Bible, where would it be? What event, what story would you most want to witness with your own eyes and ears? Would it be from the Old or New Testament? Would you observe the life and times of Jesus? Or would you seek to unravel ancient mysteries like who exactly were the Nephilim (Gen 6:4)? Would you rewind to the very beginning to behold the perfect creation (maybe even try to warn Adam and Eve)? Or would you fast-forward to the very end, the glorious new heavens and new earth? Or would you perhaps transport to one of those epic gems in between, such as the grand exodus out of Egypt?

Regardless of which story you choose, in order to truly get the most out of your time-traveling quest, you would need to grasp how that event connects to other stories *and* how it also fits into the bigger story of the Bible. It's like visiting modern-day sites of ancient ruins. How can one really appreciate marvels like Masada, the Colosseum, or the Egyptian Pyramids without knowing their vast history? Similarly, even if you were an eyewitness to a well-known event in the Bible, you would still be severely limited in your understanding of that story and its significance apart from knowing its connections to all the other stories.

It is for this reason I couldn't choose between the testaments. How could I limit myself to just one part of the story? I want the *whole* story— the big picture. But I also want all the details explained. The good news is there is in fact one such place in the Bible for my tall and complicated order. I would choose to land my time-traveling pod on the dusty road to Emmaus (Luke 24:13–35). Anticlimactic as that may be for some, it is there I would walk in step with the resurrected Messiah listening to his own interpretation of the *entire* Hebrew Scriptures (Old Testament) and how all the parts are fulfilled wholly in him:

The Story Ripples of the Bible

> Beginning with Moses and all the Prophets, he explained to them what was said in all the Scriptures concerning himself. (Luke 24:27)

How I wish these words were the opening line to another mighty sermon—the "Sermon on the Road"—full of chapters recording every explanation, every word, every jot and tittle uttered by this rabbi recently returned from the dead. But alas, the verse is a terse summary, and we can only imagine what this Bible study on-the-go was like.

Even so, like the two Emmaus-bound disciples in this chapter, I know my mind would open and my heart would burn within me as everything finally came together—past, present, and future; the mind and the heart; the human and the divine—in perfect harmony and a unity that only Jesus can bring. I would savor this simple stroll with the incarnate Word of God, listening to him expound and exegete his own words. It is the best walking with God I can imagine.

It is also on this road that so many Bible questions would find answers. But there's one large and looming question I've spent most of my life asking—a question whose answer would answer many questions about the Bible and beyond. If you chose to time travel back into the times or writings of Moses, it's likely you've wondered this question yourself. *Exactly where did Moses write about Jesus?*

Notice that Jesus begins with *Moses* in his explanations on that road: "Beginning with Moses . . ." (Luke 24:27). Jesus first explains how Moses' writings—the first five books of the Bible: Genesis, Exodus, Leviticus, Numbers, and Deuteronomy—are about him as the Messiah. In Matt 5:17, Jesus makes clear his relationship to the Hebrew Scriptures: he did not come to abolish the Law or the Prophets but to fulfill them. While the "Prophets" refers to the prophetic writings, the "Law" refers to the writings of Moses, known as the Torah or Pentateuch.

The idea of Moses writing or testifying about the Messiah is a point Jesus had emphasized repeatedly to the leaders and teachers of his day: "If you believed Moses, you would believe me; for he wrote of me" (John 5:46), and "You search the Scriptures because you think that in them you have eternal life; and it is they that bear witness about me, yet you refuse to come to me that you may have life" (John 5:39–40). But Jesus' big claims in these verses simply beg this big question: Exactly where did Moses write about Jesus?

Introduction

I think most people would agree it is far easier flipping through the prophetic writings like Isaiah, Jeremiah, Ezekiel, and others for a biblical witness of Jesus. But Moses? Even if we believe Moses did write about Jesus, can we explain to others how those books bear testimony to and find fulfillment in him? Do we understand it for ourselves?

Additionally, what exactly did a Jewish mind in Jesus' day expect or understand from Moses' writings by which to examine Jesus and conclude he was in fact the Messiah? In other words, how did a first-century Jewish mind think about the Hebrew Scriptures? Or better yet, how were they *supposed* to think—especially concerning Moses and his writings? I believe on that road to Emmaus, Jesus answered those very questions, causing the mind to expand and the heart to burn at the euphonic harmony of all the Scriptures.

But the way to a conviction of biblical harmony requires confronting perceptions of discord. So let me just go ahead and say what we're already thinking: from a simple reading of the five books of Moses, it is *not obvious* where or how Moses talks about the Messiah. Unlike the Prophets, the Pentateuch is not dripping with Messiah talk—at least, not directly or immediately and certainly not according to the typical way we think about prophecy.

In fact, according to a tally that was taken, one discovers "about nine prominent verses in the Torah that people commonly consider messianic prophecies (Gen 3:15; 49:8–12; Num 24:17–19; Deut 18:15), out of a total of 5845 verses, or less than one fourth of one percent (0.15%)."[1] And even where those messianic verses appear, they are often brief and quick, just a sudden glimpse within a fleeting text that is eager to move on. On top of that, we are still left wondering if such verses are immediately or directly about Jesus or if it is a bit more complex than that.

So again, what can it mean that Moses wrote of Jesus (John 5:46) or that the Law of Moses finds fulfillment in Jesus (Matt 5:17)? Surely the Messiah had the whole mountain of Torah in mind and not a mere nine pebbles, right? Sounds like another tall and complicated order. Thankfully, the Bible is full of good news, including answers to these puzzling questions.

---

1. Postell, *Reading Moses, Seeing Jesus*, ch. 3, "The Torah's Remedy."

The Story Ripples of the Bible

Story

It is not so much about *where* Moses wrote about the Messiah but *how*. Perhaps the biggest missing piece to our conception of messianic prophecy—how the Bible bears witness to or gets fulfilled in the Messiah—is story. Often when believers think about prophecy in the Bible, we tend to limit it to mere predictions about the future. We generally measure prophecy as direct and immediate foretellings about the Messiah, which is why we are inclined to run to and rely more heavily on the writings of the Prophets when we want to show how Jesus clearly fulfilled something. We want statements that we can reference easily and point people to quickly—statements that answer the "where" question. But this common approach is based on a perception that results in a mere nine verses concerning the Messiah in all the Torah.

While prediction is certainly one aspect, prophecy as *mere* prediction is shallow waters. You won't get very far, and there isn't as much happening at the surface. You might be the kind of person who is perfectly content sunbathing on the beach and taking a dip every once in a while. But then there are those of you who can't wait to go scuba-diving or snorkeling because it would add far more thrill and adventure to your vacation. Well, when it comes to the vast ocean of Bible prophecy, the ancient authors and prophets urge us not to get sedentary on the shallow surface. We've simply got to take the refreshing plunge into the deep in order to behold the life, beauty, and mystery of the prophetic. And like the literal ocean, these deep waters have many stories to tell.

The way prophecy works in the Bible is far more complex, layered, and poetic than what we might be used to as Western thinkers. Biblical prophecy is not only about the future; actually, it's quite the opposite! More often than not, prophecy has deep roots in Israel's ancient past. And as we will see, even the prophets themselves weren't only making predictions into the future in their writings. Most of the time, they are looking *backward* into Israel's past stories and promises in order to frame and make sense of both their own present world and events to take place in Israel's future. Tim Mackie likens the prophets to "covenant watchdogs,"[2] who exhorted God's people toward faithfulness by pointing them back to the covenants of the past,[3] which, in context, came with plenty of stories. In other words, much

---

2. Mackie, "What Prophecy Is For," 34:11.
3. Eric Tully has also stated, "The ethics of the Prophets are based on the law given

Introduction

of the prophets' prophecies poetically play on past stories in order to get across God's messages to his present-day people (and those in the future).

Most of the Bible is, believe it or not, story.[4] Most of the writings of Moses—the first five books of the Bible—is story. And everything else that is not story—such as laws, genealogies, holidays, and songs—still falls within the context of a story within the greater story of redemption.

For example, the appointed times in Lev 23—while they seem to be written solely for the purpose of law, order, and tradition within Israel's society—are primarily given to remember the stories behind these holidays. It is these stories that impart divine revelation of who God is, his heart toward his people, and his plans to execute redemption on the earth, which are the weightier matters of any law.

- The Sabbath recalls the creation story—rich in wonder, beauty, and knowledge of who God is—and his purposes for his creation (Exod 20:8–11).
- The Feast of Tabernacles is observed so that Israel remembers their story of wandering the wilderness and God's enduring presence through it all (Lev 23:42–43).
- Passover and the Feast of Unleavened Bread are all about calling to mind the story of God's mighty deliverance of his people out of Egypt (Exod 12:14). The exodus story is so central to Israel's identity and relationship with God that it not only becomes a central holiday but the rationale behind so many other laws in the Torah, such as how to treat foreigners in Israel (Lev 19:33–34).

Besides the appointed times on the Hebrew calendar, God attaches the stories of Israel to his very *name*, making himself known to both Israel and all the nations through his history with his people. In identifying himself as the God of Abraham, Isaac, and Jacob or the God of Israel, we are meant to

---

to Moses in Exodus, Leviticus, and Deuteronomy. . . . Much of the prophetic message is related in some way to the covenants that God had made in Genesis, Exodus, and 2 Samuel." Tully, *Reading the Prophets*, 4.

4. Or, as Leland Ryken puts it, "Narrative is the dominant form in the Bible." *How to Read the Bible*, 33. My use of the word "story" (or "stories") refers to the simple genre of narrative. Let the reader also understand that my use of the word "story" presupposes *history*, not fiction. I fully subscribe to the literal-grammatical-historical method of Bible interpretation. In other words, these Bible "stories" actually took place in real space and time. Additionally, I view the art of typology as part of, in harmony with, and even integral to this method of interpretation as well as the biblical author's intent.

get a sense of who God is via his personal interactions with Abraham, Isaac, Jacob, and the nation of Israel. God even says to Moses in the burning-bush encounter—after revealing himself as the God of his fathers, the God of Abraham, Isaac, and Jacob—that this is his name forever, and "thus I am to be *remembered* throughout all generations" (Exod 3:15, emphasis added).[5] Eternally etched into God's very name are continual flashbacks to the stories of Israel. This is not only a testament to how permanently and passionately God has united himself to his people, but it also teaches us about *how* to read and handle the Scriptures. We are to prioritize the dominating genre of narrative because the Bible primarily imparts knowledge of God and rich theological truths through storytelling.

In the Bible, you cannot run away from story. The Scripture tells a story through stories. But can Bible stories really function as prophecy? Not only do I wholeheartedly believe they do but that they were meant to. It is simply not possible that Jesus, in his exhaustive explanations on that road to Emmaus, left out or bypassed the genre that makes up most of the Bible—narrative. This genre is the answer to *how* Moses' writings are about the Messiah.

Therefore, in our efforts to understand how all the Scripture with all its genres testifies to Jesus, we absolutely need to reclaim story as messianic prophecy—even the root of all prophecy, as narrative makes up the core and context of every book of the Bible. Additionally, we need to beware of reducing prophecy to mere predictions that can be conveniently Westernized as a list in an Excel spreadsheet. For any disciple of this Jesus who made sense of his own life story and calling in the prophetic light of *all* the Scripture and its genres, it is imperative his disciples today, too, tread this same road with Jesus and recognize him as truly the completion and fulfillment of the whole of Scripture—every genre, every jot and tittle.

Lastly, what shall we do with all those stories that don't seem to correlate or even concern themselves with the Messiah in that direct, predictive, and immediate way we are so used to and comfortable with? We linger and listen to the Bible authors *build* their stories on their terms. Slowing down, tuning in, and persevering are big asks the ancients place upon an instant, hurried, and scrolling culture. But to them, taking time to listen to a story—with ears that actually hear—was the stuff of life. And it still is even for us.

---

[5] All italics in Scripture quotations are my addition.

Introduction

Teshuvah

Teshuvah is the Hebrew word for return or repentance. It is a word I find particularly helpful to reclaiming Bible stories as messianic prophecy because instead of constantly searching for answers in something new and innovative, it beckons us to orient ourselves toward answers that have already been supplied to us but somehow gotten lost or forgotten. The past echoes with wisdom, answers, direction, and orientation to reality:

> Thus says the Lord: "Stand by the roads, and look, and ask for the ancient paths, where the good way is; and walk in it, and find rest for your souls." (Jer 6:16)

Teshuvah helps us recover the good and true from which we have strayed, regain what we have lost, and remember what we have forgotten—for the sake of our souls. Now, the way people use and apply the concept of *teshuvah* is usually on an individual scale concerning one's personal faith and spirituality. It can also be applied on a large, national scale like in Scripture when the Lord called the entire nation of Israel to repent or when believers today pray for America to return to God.

But *teshuvah* also happens—and should happen—within academia. Within biblical scholarship, there have been all sorts of returns to the forgotten past and regaining of lost truths, including the return to the historical Jewish roots of the Christian faith, which has helped to restore Jesus back to his original Jewish context and identity.[6] Additionally, there has also been a return to the value of approaching and studying the Bible as literature, which it most certainly is! These are two excellent steps in the right direction, and they greatly inform and reform our thinking of prophecy. I believe such returns require us to rethink the Bible's stories as the main literary channel for not only extracting sound theology in general but for rightly discerning messianic prophecy—namely, the chosen path and story the Messiah was destined to walk.

---

6. Of course, these returns are by no means perfect and faultless. The quest for the historical Jesus within scholarship also produced outcomes believers would consider neither biblical nor fruitful as the movement skeptically stripped Jesus of his deity and discredited the gospels. But when we separate the chaff from the wheat of this movement, I think believers can agree that the newfound interest to dig deeper into the authentic Jewish context of a Jesus who was almost entirely buried beneath generations of later church tradition and doctrine generally proved a providential step in the right direction. For a better understanding of the quest(s) for the historical Jesus, I recommend the short essay on The Gospel Coalition's website: Bock, "Quests for the Historical Jesus."

And in reclaiming story as prophecy or rooting prophecy in story, we are returning to a more ancient, biblical, and Hebrew way of thinking about the Hebrew Bible. We are returning the text to its proper context. We are treating the Bible according to its own terms rather than imposing anachronistic, Western categories and modern demands upon it. We might want prophecy to be easy, direct, clear, and quick, but if our aim is for a faithful and deeper understanding of God's word, then these modern categories will require our *teshuvah*.

The presence of so many stories in the Bible and the fact that story is the glue binding the entire Scriptures together suggest the biblical writers were more into *showing* than *telling*. This means that the human authors (and even divine author) of the Bible spent less time making new, direct, and random predictions about the future than they did on slowly developing old and familiar types, themes, patterns, and profiles through storytelling. Their frequent flashbacks to past stories, parallels, and persons also foreshadowed the future. And as the biblical narrative progresses from the Old to the New Testament, the ripple effect of these growing patterns and recycled stories eventually expands into a silhouette ready for the Messiah to step into as its perfect match. The apostle Paul used his own analogy for this same idea in Col 2:17, calling these developing patterns the "shadow of things to come, but the substance belongs to Christ."

Now, today this technique already has a big theological term, but I think sometimes these terms can often stunt rather than support our attempt to make sense of the Scriptures. Such stumbling blocks can make the deep and rich treasures dwelling within the text hard to see and hard to reach. When we read the Scripture, our spirits are supposed to cry out "how profound Your thoughts!" (Ps 92:5, HCSB) and "How precious to me are your thoughts, O God! How vast is the sum of them! If I would count them, they are more than the sand!" (Ps 139:17–18). Or as Paul exclaims, "Oh, the depth of the riches and wisdom and knowledge of God!" (Rom 11:33). Indeed, every believer is meant to dig deep into the treasure troves of the word of God—*all* of it.

So, I'm renaming this big theological term for our journey in this book. What is known as biblical typology,[7] I'm simply calling *story ripples*—as in

---

7. This book agrees with James Hamilton's responsible approach to and detailed definition of typology in biblical studies: "God-ordained, author-intended historical correspondence and escalation in significance between people, events, and institutions across the Bible's redemptive-historical story" (Hamilton, *Typology*, 26). There is also narrative analogy, which is prominent in Jewish/Israeli scholarship of the Hebrew Bible.

Introduction

a ripple effect, which I think provides helpful imagery for capturing the movement of developing themes and patterns observed in the biblical stories.

We all know that when you drop an object in a still body of water it has a natural ripple effect. It begins with one small ripple that repeats over and over again while also expanding larger and larger as time passes. These future ripples are, in a way, foreshadowed by the previous ones. In other words, you know they're coming! You expect the ripples to grow and expand even further into the future. Every ripple connects to and looks similar to all the others, but each individual ripple is still different, bigger, and unique in the surface area it covers at that specific moment in time. These ever-expanding ripples are set into unceasing motion from a single drop to eventually engulf the entire body of water, leaving no part untouched by its transforming frequencies.

Bible stories are like that. Just as an object sets off a current of recycling, ever-expanding ripples in a body of water, so God set off a current of story ripples in history. And as these stories—along with their embedded themes and imagery—expectantly advance into the future, they grow and develop, touching and transforming the entire body of Scripture. Each ripple is meant to serve as both a flashback and a foreshadowing. They make us remember the previous ripples, and they also set the stage for another similar yet more advanced ripple in the future.

Now, while I love this analogy for the unique way it captures the movement behind biblical themes and stories, it is still limited. It does not, for example, provide us with a final big picture (of Jesus) that we get with the analogy of a tapestry or a portrait that are slowly put together by individual threads or strokes. But as the American poet Robert Frost wisely discerned, "all metaphor breaks down somewhere."[8] And this is certainly true when trying to capture the complex and creative genius behind the biblical text.

Jonathan Grossman defines narrative analogy as an "intentional literary device which creates a dialogue between two texts, a figurative device that the author uses to express hidden meanings, and through which the reader is invited to reveal them: In many cases in Scripture, the closeness of motifs (and also in language) is so obvious between the two stories that one cannot escape the conclusion that one of its authors knew the other story and used it as bricks in the building of his story" (see Grossman's definition in Postell, "Reading Genesis, Seeing Moses," 437). The idea behind "story ripples" draws from both typology and narrative analogy. For more on the latter, see Postell's articles "Learning from Israeli Scholars" and "Reading Genesis, Seeing Moses."

8. Frost, "Education by Poetry," 723.

The point is that Bible prophecy is not only direct and predictive such as Daniel having a vision about the immediate and messianic future (Dan 10-12). Prophecy is also progressively demonstrated through narrative. The biblical nature of storytelling is to move slowly and build strategically toward something—or someone. And only in the final stage do you piece together the grand picture and purpose, although glimpses can be experienced along the way.

Bible stories sew in one thread or theme that then gets connected and interconnected to other threads and ripples to form a pattern among other patterns, all of which come together and only make sense with the finished product. The Bible as a whole weaves together a tapestry of the Messiah, and it does so mainly through stories.

As I said, the biblical writers were more into showing than telling. By the way, Jesus did this all the time. When asked "Who is my neighbor?" by an expert in the Law of Moses, Jesus *showed* his answer with the story of the good Samaritan (Luke 10:25-37). Jesus didn't reference or explain a law from the Torah or even tell him directly "Your neighbor is the one you see in need, your fellow Jew, but also your perceived enemy like the Samaritans." His preferred method of communication—namely, storytelling—demonstrates this ancient Jewish tradition and inclination to show instead of tell. Besides the parables, Jesus frequently taught and responded to the religious teachers of his day with Bible stories: Adam and Eve (Matt 19:3-6); Noah, Lot, and Lot's wife (Luke 17:26-33); Moses (John 3:14-15); David (Matt 12:2-4); the queen of the South and Solomon (Matt 12:42); Jonah (Matt 12:38-41); Elijah and Elisha (Luke 4:25-27).

Likewise, the Bible—as ancient Jewish literature—is written to uncover and discover. It does not lecture you or throw knowledge at you. It is not a classroom environment. It is a conversation on the road inviting you to walk and wrestle with truth for yourself. It pulls you in to taste and see the Lord's goodness for yourself and to share in the adventures and experiences of long ago. And it accomplishes this best through storytelling—and story ripples. Like Jesus' followers on the road to Emmaus, we must learn to slow down and listen to the biblical authors narrating and connecting their stories because, through them, they are showing us something important and transformative—prophetic even. Within those stories, we discover purposefully embedded messianic prophecy and capture God's vision for the future. And when we better understand how the Bible moves toward Messiah, our hearts and lives will, too.

Introduction

Literary Devices

Now, you might ask, exactly how does the Bible use story to inspire and build prophecy? Great question! The Bible comes packaged in all sorts of literary devices like metaphor and irony but especially flashbacks, foreshadowing, parallels, repetition, and patterns to other stories, events, and people that we've seen before. So in reading major events or people in biblical stories, there is very often going to be a flashback to a similar past event/person and a foreshadowing to a future event/person. In this way, we discover both the author's agenda and the divine agency behind the text. James E. Allman says, "Biblical narrative revolves around patterns intentionally embedded in the story . . . that the human authors and the divine Author expected even the original readers to recognize and understand."[9] Yair Zakovitch also insists that the biblical narrators "expect a high level of sophistication" from their readers; they expect one who "absorbs the links and discerns the relationship between stories."[10]

As mentioned earlier, even when it comes to the directly messianic and predictive prophecies in the prophets—such as the Messiah being born in Bethlehem or of a virgin—we have to realize that prophets like Isaiah and Jeremiah were not only and always receiving completely new revelations. Often, the prophetic "word of the Lord" still came in the context of a familiar storyline and ripples that God set into motion long ago. In their eyes, many of these prophecies and revelations would have served as a new development of a previous ripple, pattern, or promise from the past. After all, the prophets were still working with the Scriptures they knew. And in those Scriptures, they would have known Bethlehem served as the humble town where the great King David was born; therefore, it makes complete sense that the Son of David and King of Kings would follow in that same ancient pattern. The great prophets also would have been long familiar with the supernatural sign that a miraculous birth proved. After all, the entire nation of Israel (and so many other important figures within Israel) was birthed out of the impossibility of a barren woman bearing a child. Stories with this theme get featured over and over again from Genesis all the way to the New Testament.

---

9. Quoted in Rydelnik and Blum, *Moody Handbook*, 382–83. A good, in-depth resource for exploring this point further is Hamilton's *Typology*, 17–28.
10. Zakovitch, "Through the Looking Glass," 152.

The Story Ripples of the Bible

Especially for the prophecies considered heavily messianic (and that later get quoted in the gospels), the prophets often worked with ancient stories and established patterns in Israel's history that they retold, recast, and reframed in divinely inspired ways for their generation. These prophets were thinking in terms of precedented ripples, not psychic knowledge. The prophets were not like the fortune-telling mediums of Israel's surrounding nations, and Bible prophecy is not magic. Prophetic revelation revolves around divinely-established ancient patterns in the context of a familiar story and covenant relationship. And flashbacks to this past story and relationship have a foreshadowing element to them that forms the future. The biblical authors wrote to "[instruct] their readers about how to live for the future, following patterns of relationship to God that are revealed in their historical accounts."[11] This is the complex, circular, and covenantal nature of sacred messianic prophecy. It's hardly ever a foretelling of the future in a way that is isolated from the past. The past is also about the future. The past has everything to do with the future and the present. The prophets interpreted and made sense of both their present day and the future of Israel through past stories and patterns. Therefore, the past, present, and future are all intimately connected in the world of biblical literature and messianic prophecy. Truly, it is a beautiful thing to behold.

Israel

I believe that recovering story as messianic prophecy is not only more in line with the way the original Hebrew mind would have conceived about the coming Messiah, but it recaptures the centrality of Israel in the Bible and in God's plan of redemption, which is still an enormous missing piece in the Western Christian mind. Too often today, the gospel gets presented through four main stages in the biblical overview: creation, fall, redemption in Jesus, and consummation, thereby skipping entirely over Israel's history and what God was doing there. But Israel's history is precisely where we see God crafting the blueprint and categories of his plan for world restoration—through stories! God's relationship with Israel (which literally makes up the rest of the Bible after Gen 11) is indeed a weighty thing to leave out or skip over, whether it be in our witness or personal understanding of the Bible. One can't remove the heart and still expect the blood to flow throughout the body. By doing away with the story of Israel, we also do away with the

11. Mitchell, *Message of the Psalter*, 84–85.

INTRODUCTION

weightiness of our witness as we cut off the flow of the Scriptures toward Jesus. I dare say, ignorance on this matter is also not something any follower of Jesus can afford in their walk with God. Grasping Jesus as the fulfillment of all the Scripture is the cement solidifying all other convictions of the faith, whether personal or communal.

Rediscovering the prophetic current within Bible stories also returns the Messiah to his people—his kinsmen according to the flesh—and regards him as inseparable from them. He is not only one of them, but he actually walks in their very footsteps. When Jesus arrived, his story retraced and relived the story of all Israel as well as key individuals who themselves received the privilege of foreshadowing the face and footsteps of the Messiah and his message—people like Abraham, Joseph, Moses, David, Esther, and others. Jesus fulfilled the Scriptures by sharing in the stories of his people.

I believe this kind of thinking makes up much of what Jesus himself had in mind when he made statements like, "Believe me that I am in the Father and the Father is in me, or else believe on account of the works themselves" (John 14:11). What works? Works, signs, and wonders that were already expected, prophesied, staged, and patterned on the stories and history of Israel. I believe Jesus wanted people to see and know that he did not come on his own authority or do anything by his own authority. He came treading the well-beaten path of Israel's story and as the continuation of that story. He came to accomplish what was already promised, patterned, and prophesied.

Additionally, while Jesus' arrival inaugurated the new covenant of new life, a new creation, and a new heart, he did not start his own new and separate religion. A reformer brings new and timely developments, but he does so as an insider standing on the authority of some precedent or pattern already established. None of what Jesus did was isolated from Israel's past. Rather, he was in submission to the ancient story and their prophetic ripples; he came as their fulfillment, as the long-awaited resolution to a great conflict within a great story. That fulfillment would certainly bring about drastic new changes, such as the adoption of a new family member, the gentiles (Eph 2:19). But the inclusion of the nations was a ripple that got its prophetic start all the way back in Genesis with Abraham, not with Jesus or the book of Acts.

Now, in order to catch the ripples connecting the works of Jesus and God's works in the Old Testament, we must dive into some of the aforementioned literary features of the biblical text. That dive, however, does

The Story Ripples of the Bible

not need to be a deep and intense academic scrutiny of every literary facet of the Bible. It is sufficient to cover just a few key literary devices—simple ones you'll likely know or remember from your high school English class—techniques like flashbacks, foreshadowing, repetition, parallels, and comparisons. These will serve as portals big enough to open our eyes to the Scriptures and cause our hearts to burn as we explore how key stories from Moses to the prophets build up the portrait and testimony of Messiah Jesus.

As you read this book, please note a few things:

1. While this book makes literary and theological connections between multiple biblical texts, it features only a selective sampling. This book is intended as more of an introductory than exhaustive treatment of Bible ripples. That means I do not address every reference where a story, pattern, or theme in the Bible gets picked up by the authors and recycled in a new way. I do, however, connect key Bible passages from the Torah (Pentateuch), the Prophets/Writings, and the New Testament for each story ripple I explore. You will see those references at the beginning of each chapter, and I encourage you to linger a bit in those passages (and not skip over them) before diving into the study.

2. In some chapters, I digress from "ripples" and employ simple parallels to more meticulously compare the life and patterns of one individual (like Moses) directly to Jesus without tracing other Moses-like figures or ripples throughout the Old Testament. While ripples zoom out to recognize bigger connections across the whole story of Scripture, parallelism zooms in to behold connections in the details. For good Bible study, you absolutely need both.

3. Finally, since there are so many other patterns and ripples I do not cover in this book,[12] they remain to be traced by you! I hope this book will inspire you to pick up a Bible dictionary, concordance, commentary, perhaps one of the books mentioned in the footnotes/bibliography, or simply the Bible alone and see what prophetic currents you discover.[13] A key rule to remember for detecting either past or future

---

12. This includes end-times prophecy, which I have intentionally left out (with one, brief exception in chapter Joseph) so as to allow readers to immerse in this primary and foundational grasping of prophecy, where Jesus brings fulfillment and remains at the center, not us or our current events. Only when one examines the relationship between the past, present, and future *within* the biblical text can he or she be equipped to grapple with prophecy that yet remains to be fulfilled.

13. I say this with caution. While the Spirit can and does reveal biblical connections

Introduction

ripples is "shared vocabulary and syntax" (the arrangement of words in a sentence) as well as "shared structure and sequence" (of ideas).[14] Look out for "plots with similar themes and which are constructed in parallel or similar fashion," as this will help protect against being "carried away by coincidental associations" between two stories.[15] Equally important to remember is that while ripples share similarities, they are not the exact same. So be open and allow for differences, developments, and departing twists—all of which are also present and purposeful. Where necessary, I address these.

You

There remains one last but vital point to mention. These ripples do not only serve as a powerful and divine witness to the authenticity of the Scriptures themselves, the fluid harmony between the Hebrew Scriptures and the New Testament, and to the vindication of Jesus as the Messiah sent by God. The cool thing about the story ripples of the Bible is that they also move into our lives and flow into our souls today. God did not only develop these ripples into the stories of the Bible, but he continues to extend and expand them into our stories. "The power of story as a literary form is its uncanny ability to involve us in what is happening."[16] "The natural function of narrative is to help the reader hear the voices, take part in the action, get involved in the plot."[17]

There is no other book out there where the reader not only gets involved in the story but also gets invited to become part of the story. More on this later, but you should know that as a believer united to Jesus, your life and testimony are pulled into the Bible's ripple effect. As you read this book, keep in the back of your mind your own experiences and encounters with the Lord and his word (just make sure these remain in the *back,* and

---

using the word of God alone, we should also glean from God's work in and through others who have poured over the Scriptures and studied certain subjects longer and harder than most. Typology is one such subject that calls for careful study and biblical grounding. A helpful and easy-to-read resource for questions and concerns about typology and how to engage with it responsibly is Chase, *40 Questions*.

14. Schnittjer and Harmon, *How to Study*, 62–63.
15. Zakovitch, "Through the Looking Glass," 139–40.
16. Ryken, *How to Read the Bible*, 34.
17. Perrin, *New Testament*, 165.

try to resist the urge of bringing your experiences to the immediate front and bypassing the first and original meaning of the text).

Ultimately, the hope is for you to connect the details of how God first worked the ripples of his stories and his Son off the pages of his Book and into your own life story, into your heart, soul, and mind. It is important and helpful to know that you and your story are caught in the current that now reverberates God's story and his Son into the future. And while your story doesn't hold the same "divine inspiration" that characterizes the sacred Scriptures, you nevertheless have become a walking witness of his Book by the divine work and inspiration of the same Holy Spirit. Through the phenomenon of story, you have come to share in experiences patterned long ago, thereby becoming part of the cloud of great witnesses. There is great comfort and reassuring strength to be gained from knowing the path you are walking is well trodden. "Oh, the depth of the . . . wisdom and knowledge of God!" (Rom 11:33).

My heart in writing this book is to fuel your heart to burn within you at the opening of your mind to the treasures of Scripture—treasures both old and new. No need to sit long hours in gloomy study halls or climb high philosophical ivory towers. Simply take a conversational stroll with Jesus on your own Emmaus road.

Jesus, you are our rabbi, our teacher. As we open and discuss your Scriptures, come alongside us as you did those two disciples and open our minds to behold the poetic beauty and complex wonder of how the writings of Moses and the Prophets come together in you. Help us to recognize you as not just a prophet powerful in word and deed but as the risen Messiah of Israel and redeemer of all nations.

Chapter Abraham

STORY RIPPLE: DISINHERITANCE AND REGRAFTING

Now the Lord said to Abram, "Go from your country and your kindred and your father's house to the land that I will show you. And I will make of you a great nation, and I will bless you and make your name great, so that you will be a blessing. I will bless those who bless you, and him who dishonors you I will curse, and in you all the families of the earth shall be blessed." —Genesis 12:1–3

I am the Lord; I have called you in righteousness; I will take you by the hand and keep you; I will give you as a covenant for the people, a light for the nations. —Isaiah 42:6

It is too small a thing for you to be my servant to restore the tribes of Jacob and bring back those of Israel I have kept. I will also make you a light for the Gentiles, that my salvation may reach to the ends of the earth. —Isaiah 49:6 NIV

And Jesus came up and spoke to them, saying, "All authority in heaven and on earth has been given to Me. Go, therefore, and make disciples of all the nations, baptizing them in the name of the Father and the Son and the Holy Spirit, teaching them to follow all that I commanded you; and behold, I am with you always, to the end of the age." —Matt 28:18–20 NASB

PERHAPS IT IS UNUSUAL for such a book to begin with Abraham and his call rather than at the beginning with Adam and the creation. It is not

The Story Ripples of the Bible

unusual, however, for authors—ancient and modern—to intentionally open their stories and plots in the middle of some action (this is a literary device known as *in medias res*—Latin for "in the middle of things"—for any fellow nerds out there). Grabbing the reader's attention with unexpected disorientation is an excellent set up and powerful tool to then gradually fill in the holes through flashbacks and foreshadowing, which serve to give readers those ever so satisfying "aha" moments. Films do this all the time, especially to help viewers make key connections between the past, present, and future as they piece together the full story. As modern readers of the ancient Scriptures, this literary perspective can often prove more helpful to making key connections than if we started at the expected beginning.

Much of the Bible contains flashbacks to the past that shed perspective on the present while foreshadowing the future all at the same time. And as we shall see later on, the biblical prophets are themselves writers whose books open by plunging their readers in the middle of a drama series, assuming their audience is already well versed in the grand story from its beginning.[1] So the more we understand the Bible's beginning stories, the more we will experience those wonderful "aha" connections when coming across an allusion or flashback in the prophets.[2]

By the time the storyline of the Bible arrives at God's call of Abraham in Gen 12, the reader has just stumbled upon a major milestone in biblical history. And, although centuries apart, the parallel milestone of Gen 12 is Matt 28, Jesus' Great Commission to his disciples. These two milestones mirror each other in incredible ways that only God can accomplish. It is immensely important for Bible readers to grasp just how connected and momentous these milestones are in the plan of redemption. But to understand how the call of Abraham serves as a major milestone, we must understand what first prompted God to select this individual and create an entirely new nation out of him and his wife. Why did God go about this particular plan of salvation in the first place?

---

1. "First, the Old Testament Prophets are often difficult for us because they assume that the reader is well acquainted with all that came before in God's dealings with Israel and his revealed word. . . . The Prophets are just one part of a grand theological vision given to us in Scripture. They do not start at the beginning and catch us up. When we enter a prophetic book, we are stepping into the middle of a discussion already in progress." Tully, *Reading the Prophets*, 4.

2. "Much of the prophetic message is related in some way to the covenants that God had made in Genesis, Exodus, and 2 Samuel. The more we understand the rest of the Old Testament, the more these theological references will be obvious and make sense." Tully, *Reading the Prophets*, 4.

Chapter Abraham

For this, we need to grapple with what exactly was happening throughout Gen 1–11. We know God created Adam and Eve and called them to fill and cultivate the earth (Gen 1:28). We also know the fall happened in Gen 3. The key theme to remember in the history following the fall is that evil increases and permeates everything, compromising God's original good creation. It goes from bad to worse. The other theme to remember is that, throughout the whole time, God keeps offering a new chance to the next generation to choose life, to choose walking with him. But like their ancestors in the garden of Eden, people keep choosing death, destruction, godlessness, and evil instead of walking with God in true life. We keep rejecting the Tree of Life.

Now, exactly who are these people to whom God is offering chance after chance after chance? Notice there are no real "chosen people" or a "chosen nation" at this time. Rather, the story encompasses all people—all the descendants of Adam and Eve. And as early as Cain and Abel, God implores them to walk with him and to choose life and what is right—the same offer he gave to humanity's first parents (Gen 2:16–17). God tells Cain he must master sin that crouches at the door (Gen 4:7) in order to choose life. But Cain doesn't. And neither do his descendants. Already falling into the pattern of Adam and Eve, they all give into sin and increase it exponentially. Genesis 6 begins by telling us that when people began to multiply on the earth, "the LORD saw that the wickedness of man was great in the earth, and that every intention of the thoughts of his heart was only evil continually" (6:5). The next verse says the LORD was "sorry" to have made humankind and that "He was grieved in His heart" (6:6 NASB).

People's wickedness gets so bad that God judges the world with a flood. Even then, even after that great judgment and after God's renewal of the original Edenic promises to Noah (Gen 9:1–11), evil persists. People still won't walk with God. What's worse, the evil after the flood seems to be going in the same increasing direction as before the flood, reaching yet another climax and judgment in Gen 11 with the Tower of Babel.[3]

Like the wickedness before the flood, this tower is a picture of sheer, complete refusal and resistance to God, his terms, his ways, his life, and his *name*.[4] The crux of humanity's evil and rebellion against God is observed

---

3. "The biblical writer wastes no time in linking this act [to build the tower] to the earlier divine transgression of Genesis 6:1–4." Heiser, *Unseen Realm*, 114–115.

4. "The building of the tower of Babel meant perpetuating Babylonian religious knowledge and substituting the rule of Babel's gods for rule by Yahweh." Heiser, *Unseen Realm*, 115.

in Gen 11:4—"Come, let us build ourselves a city, with a tower that reaches to the heavens, *so that we may make a name for ourselves*" (NIV). God's image-bearers insist on making a name for themselves instead of representing God's name, as they were created to do. Although the text doesn't mention it again, we can imagine God's grief here—a double portion. But even in his sorrow, God remains steadfast in his mission to renew the original blessings and life given in the garden.

Keeping to his promise to never flood the earth again, God delivers a judgment at Babel that we first glimpsed with Adam and Eve (Gen 3:24) and will see repeated throughout the rest of the Bible: scattering. This becomes one of the key ways we observe God punishing in the Bible. We see it with Israel later (Deut 28:64; Ps 44:11; Jer 9:16; Ezek 12:15), but first we see it here at Babel. God scatters the families of the earth so that they turn into different nations, each with a different language. It is an interesting judgment because it is not a death blow, like the flood. In fact, it is a punishment that mercifully *preserves* life for those deserving death. Like Cain, whose punishment was to wander the earth like a fugitive after murdering his brother (Gen 4:10–12), the death-deserving, disobedient nations are preserved by being scattered over the earth.

Merciful as it is, it is judgment nonetheless. The punishment at Babel is an epic turning point in history because this is where we see God disinheriting the nations and choosing to do things differently.[5] That's right, the nations of the earth were once God's inheritance. And he called and called and called to them, but there was no response. So now, instead of focusing on all the nations of the earth, God decides to create and raise up an entirely new nation, and that is why we have the call of Abraham in the very next chapter (Gen 12), right after the Tower of Babel (Gen 11). And there in chapter 12, we see that one of God's blessings to Abraham is to make his *name* great (12:2). God is going to raise up a new, nonexistent people whose name and image will represent his great name.

Did God give up on the nations? Did he reject them? He certainly punishes and disinherits them. The late Michael Heiser referred to Babel as the Rom 1 event of the Old Testament.[6] Romans 1 is where we observe—with trembling!—God giving over unrepentant people to the sinful desires of their heart:

---

5. Heiser, *Unseen Realm*, 113.
6. Heiser, *Unseen Realm*, 113.

Chapter Abraham

For since the creation of the world God's invisible qualities—his eternal power and divine nature—have been clearly seen, being understood from what has been made, so that people are without excuse. For although they knew God, they neither glorified him as God nor gave thanks to him, but their thinking became futile and their foolish hearts were darkened. Although they claimed to be wise, they became fools and exchanged the glory of the immortal God for *images made to look like a mortal human being and birds and animals and reptiles.* Therefore *God gave them over* in the sinful desires of their hearts to sexual impurity for the degrading of their bodies with one another. They exchanged the truth about God for a lie, and *worshiped and served created things* rather than the Creator—who is forever praised. Amen. (Rom 1:20–25 NIV)

Whom does this sound like? The disinherited nations. In fact, Deut 4:19 warns Israel not to worship the sun and moon and stars, "things that the LORD your God has allotted to all the peoples under the whole heaven."[7] This idea of allotting to the nations false idolatrous worship is the punishment of God,[8] giving them up to their headstrong, persistent sin and the desires of their sick and deceitful hearts. So at Babel, God gives the nations over to their idolatry, false worship, and lawlessness.[9] And that's why from here on after Babel and the call of Abraham, the storyline of the rest of the Bible is staged between Israel and the nations—and the God of Israel against the other false gods of the nations.[10]

So, did God reject the nations? This truly is one of the hardest concepts of the Bible to wrap our minds and hearts around. I'm not going to minimize the difficulty of it. In fact, there are many places in the Scripture where God gets so angry that he talks about wiping out, abandoning, and divorcing—yes, even his own people![11] The language of Scripture can be extreme, emotional, and even graphic at times.

---

7. Heiser, *Unseen Realm*, 114.

8. Heiser, *Unseen Realm*, 114.

9. Another place the Bible revisits this ripple between the disobedient nations and the chosenness of Abraham/Israel is in Esau and Jacob. The brothers are basically this ripple effect personified. Their story and relationship are a flashback to the disinheritance of the nations (which gets repeated in Esau when he gives up his birthright and inheritance for a bowl of stew (Gen 25:29–34)) and the chosenness of Abraham (which gets repeated in Jacob, who cares about the inheritance and pursues God's blessing (Gen 27)).

10. Heiser, *Unseen Realm*, 115.

11. "I gave faithless Israel her certificate of divorce and sent her away because of all her adulteries" (Jer 3:8).

Genesis 6:6 records that God was so grieved and heartbroken that he regretted making mankind. It seems like when it comes to God's punishment in Scripture, it is very serious and irreversible; but thankfully, we also see punishment distributed in temporary measure. Even as God punished Adam and Eve in Gen 3, exiling them from Eden and banishing them from his presence, he made plans for their redemption in the same breath. Genesis 3:15 mixes good news within bad news. The coming of one who will crush the serpent's head is hope uttered within a proclamation of curses. And much of the Bible is written in this way, where the hope of good news or restoration mingles within the same prophetic breath uttering destruction and judgment.[12]

Similarly, in the very next chapter following God's disinheritance and scattering of the nations, God is already making plans to win back the punished-yet-preserved nations through Abraham. "And in you all the families of the earth will be blessed" (Gen 12:3 NASB). Clearly, God still has great blessings in store for the nations he just punished and scattered. And as we see later, especially in Isa 42:6,[13] the entire nation of Israel is given by God as a covenant to whom? To the nations, the long lost prodigal son. And when Israel first became a nation under Moses, their mission—that's right, Jewish people were the first evangelists!—was to be a light to the nations, a city on a hill, "a covenant for the people" (Isa 42:6) to win back the disobedient nations.

So, despite the despair of disinheritance, God made a way to re-inherit the nations again one day. This is a consistent pattern observed throughout the Bible even when it comes to Israel's own disobedience. Though God's wrath may justly rage—and though he may punish, exile,

---

12. Just a few verses after the divorce papers issued in Jer 3:8 (NIV), God proclaims in verse 12, "'Return, faithless Israel,' declares the LORD, 'I will frown on you no longer, for I am faithful,' declares the LORD, 'I will not be angry forever'" and also verse 14, "'Return, faithless people,' declares the LORD, 'for I am your husband.'"

13. One might object that this verse and even chapter refers only to Jesus, but the apostle Paul appeals to Isaiah's phrase "a light to the Gentiles" (Isa 49:6) in Acts 13:47 to refer to the Lord's personal command in his own life to preach the good news to the gentiles. How can Paul apply this Old Testament text so personally to his own life? Paul is able to do this because being a light to the nations is a ripple, one that began with Abraham and his descendants, the nation of Israel. Ultimately, this ripple gets fulfilled in Jesus, but this fulfillment doesn't take away the fact that God also used his covenantal people (both in the past and future) to shine his light and build his name among the nations.

and scatter—steadfast love and undeserved mercy form the blueprint of his unthwarted plans to regraft, reunite, and redeem.

And we, readers, taste bits and pieces of this regrafting mission first in biblical Israel's history. The people who came out of Egypt were actually a "mixed multitude" (Exod 12:38). In other words, not all who left Egypt were descendants of Jacob. We also know about the Canaanite woman Rahab and her family (Josh 6:25) and Ruth the Moabite (Ruth 1:16; 2:12) who were both integrated or grafted into Israel. Moreover, echoing the mixed multitude in Egypt, many non-Jews became Jews on Purim in Esther's day. Did you know that? Here we see another great deliverance and grafting in of yet another mixed multitude. Esther 8:17 says, "Many people of other nationalities became Jews because fear of the Jews had seized them."

But just like the nations' disinheritance climaxed at the Tower of Babel, the nations' re-inheritance climaxed in the Great Commission: "go and make disciples of all nations" (Matt 28:19 NIV)—which is still taking place to this very day! The promise to Abraham (Gen 12:3) and Israel's national mission to be a light for the nations both find their ultimate fulfillment in the Great Commission, the regathering of the once scattered people from every tongue, tribe, and nation. *The Great Commission is the redemptive reversal of Babel.*

James confirms this ultimate fulfillment in Acts 15 when he gets up to speak at the Jerusalem Council. Notice the words he uses:

> Simon [Peter] has described to us how God first intervened to choose a people for his name *from the Gentiles*. The words of the prophets are in agreement with this, as it is written: "After this I will return and rebuild David's fallen tent . . . that the rest of mankind may seek the Lord, *even all the Gentiles* who bear my name, says the Lord, who does these things'—things known from long ago"(14–18 NIV).

Long ago indeed! The gentile nations have gone from a scattered people making a name for themselves way back in Gen 11 to a redeemed people for God's name in Matt 28 and Acts 15.

Ironically, today we are living in the days when the gentiles grafted from every tongue, tribe, and nation are also commissioned to be a light to the very people that first evangelized them. As Paul states in Rom 11:11, salvation has come to the nations to make the Jewish people jealous and win them back to God. Just as it was given to Abraham to be a blessing to the nations, so now it is given to the global church—people from every tribe, tongue, and nation—to bless the children of Abraham with the light of Messiah. Just as Israel's mission was to be a light of the knowledge of God to the lost nations, so now Christians are to radiate the Light of the World to the lost sheep of the house of Israel. It is a formidable reverse parallel from biblical history to the modern day.

So you see, whether Jewish or gentile, we are all in the same boat. At one point or other in history, we have all been where the other has been. And this is precisely how Paul concludes in Rom 11: "For just as you [the gentile nations] once were disobedient to God, but now have been shown mercy because of their [Israel's] disobedience, so these also now have been disobedient, that because of the mercy shown to you [the nations] they also may now be shown mercy. For God has shut up all in disobedience, so that He may show mercy to all. Oh, the depth of the riches, both of the wisdom and knowledge of God! How unsearchable are His judgments and unfathomable His ways!" (NASB).

In conclusion, here are some summary points and other fascinating parallels:

1. From Genesis to the gospels, there is a coming *out from* the pagan nations with the call of Abraham and a going *back to* the pagan nations with the disciples in the Great Commission. Within this movement develops the mission to reclaim the earth under the rulership of God (that was lost back in Eden)—first with the land of Israel and then to the ends of the earth.

2. Abraham's mission is to begin a line of descendants that would grow into a great nation for God. And Jesus' mission is to begin a line of disciples that would grow into a global family for God.

3. Abraham and Sarah serve as a second kind of Adam and Eve. God preserves the original promises in the garden through them. And the seed of Abraham is to serve as an example of a new kind of humanity, a set-apart creation—a kingdom of priests, a holy nation. Likewise, Jesus is the last Adam and a better Abraham, for his offspring is indeed a new creation, a holy people, one new humanity. So the more we go forward in history, the more we regain the original blessings given in the garden until they reach their fullest expression in the garden-city (Rev 21–22).

4. Just like Abraham is given a land by God—a ripple of the original garden given to Adam and Eve—so God gives Jesus, the last Adam

and better Abraham, not just a garden, not just a promised land, and not even just the inherited nations (according to Ps 2:8: "Ask of me and I will give you the nations as your inheritance"). Jesus is given all authority in heaven and on earth (Matt 28:18). Jesus reclaims for God Jewish people, gentiles from every nation, and the whole creation. Both Jews and gentiles are chosen; both are finally reunited again as one family under one God.

What can we say to all this except what Paul has already exclaimed: "Oh, the depth of the riches, both of the wisdom and knowledge of God! How unsearchable are His judgments and unfathomable His ways!" (Rom 11:33 NASB).

The Story Ripples of the Bible

STORY RIPPLE: FROM BARREN TO BEARING

The Lord said, "I will surely return to you about this time next year, and Sarah your wife shall have a son." And Sarah was listening at the tent door behind him. Now Abraham and Sarah were old, advanced in years. The way of women had ceased to be with Sarah. So Sarah laughed to herself, saying, "After I am worn out, and my lord is old, shall I have pleasure?" The Lord said to Abraham, "Why did Sarah laugh and say, 'Shall I indeed bear a child, now that I am old?' *Is anything too hard for the Lord?* At the appointed time I will return to you, about this time next year, and Sarah shall have a son." But Sarah denied it, saying, "I did not laugh," for she was afraid. He said, "No, but you did laugh." —Genesis 18:10–15

In her deep anguish Hannah prayed to the Lord, weeping bitterly. And she made a vow, saying, "Lord Almighty, if you will only look on your servant's misery and remember me, and not forget your servant but give her a son, then I will give him to the Lord for all the days of his life, and no razor will ever be used on his head." —1 Samuel 1:10–11, NIV

The barren has borne seven, but she who has many children is forlorn.
—1 Samuel 2:5

And behold, your relative Elizabeth in her old age has also conceived a son, and this is the sixth month with her who was called barren. *For nothing will be impossible with God.* —Luke 1:36–37

The ripple we're going to examine here is the strategy God chooses to make good on his promise to Abraham: "I will make of you a great nation" (Gen 12:2). His strategy? Mission impossible. The Lord literally raises up a nation by confronting the impossible head on. As readers, we pick up on this central mission and theme from the words God directs at Sarah: "Is anything too hard for the Lord?" (Gen 18:14). Truth or dare?

The first and main way we see God implementing his daring strategy—his mission impossible—is by blessing the barren woman with a child. We first see this miracle with Sarah, the first matriarch of Israel, and from there it becomes a central and familiar pattern throughout Scripture. Perhaps most importantly, this barren-to-bearing pattern will serve as a chief sign alerting the ancient Israelites that God is on the move—that he is about to do something big and pivotal. It serves as a sign from God because of how impossible it is, but also because the God of Israel is known for doing the impossible. That is the reputation he is determined to build among the nations through Abraham and Sarah. Through the backdrop of their weaknesses and impossibilities, God is going to make a name for himself, one that will turn heads and drop the jaws of nations.

After Sarah, we see this barren-to-bearing theme really taking off and developing all throughout biblical history. It's almost like a gene that gets passed down, starting with the immediate family. Isaac's wife, Rebekah, also finds herself barren (Gen 25:21); but, like Sarah, God's promise for blessing passes down to her, too. Eventually Rebekah's important children will continue to reveal God is on the move doing something momentous. When Esau and Jacob are born, they arrive as key figures not only to the birth of the nation of Israel, but Jacob and Esau serve as a prophetic picture of the relationship between Israel and the nations, which we covered in the previous ripple and will return to in the next chapter.

After Isaac, it comes as no surprise that Jacob's wife—his beloved Rachel—finds herself barren (Gen 29:31). But when she finally gives birth to Joseph, she births a key biblical character who will prove pivotal to the survival and salvation of all Israel (Gen 50:20) and whose unique experiences will serve as the foundational story framing the gospel of reconciliation and the Messiah's own profile. We will also read more about this in the next chapter on Joseph.

With each new impossible situation of barrenness in each of the great matriarchs of the faith, God is unraveling his plan of redemption and solidifying his reputation as the God of hope against all the odds. This is the God with whom nothing will be impossible, nothing will be too hard. Judaism and the Jewish people were founded upon this daring principle and divine reputation. And with every new promise that unfolds in Israel's history, it is as though the conversation between God and Sarah never stopped. Each promise that gets birthed into being through the impossible serves as a clear, never-ending answer to God's question for Sarah: "Is anything too hard for the LORD?" (Gen 18:14).

We hear reverberations of this ancient question even in the modern state of Israel's national anthem called HaTikvah ("The Hope"), which recounts:

> As long as the Jewish spirit is yearning deep in the heart,

With eyes turned toward the East, looking toward Zion,
Then our hope—the two-thousand-year-old hope—will not be lost.[14]

It is more than two thousand years old, in fact. The hope began here with the first Jewish matriarch, Sarah. Such ancient hope is not lost because the God of Israel is the God of hope against impossible odds. And for the eye that turns toward this God, hope is revived and obstacles are overcome, even miraculously.

While the Bible features other important births from barrenness (Samson in Judg 13:2–5 and the Shunammite's son whom Elisha resurrects in 2 Kgs 4:8–44), the next pivotal event I will discuss where God blesses a barren woman with a child is Hannah, the mother of Samuel. Samuel is born to be a significant judge, prophet, and forerunner who prepares Israel for their first king and the coming kingdom. In fact, in Hannah's song, we encounter the Hebrew word for messiah, *mashiach*, although it is translated "anointed" (1 Sam 2:10). God is once again on the move, advancing his divine plan and promises of redemption to the next stage. Samuel is the one who gets to identify and anoint the great King David (1 Sam 16:12–13), the king who sets up the royal profile for God's chosen messiah and who establishes the (literal) kingdom in Israel—a united kingdom of peace (2 Sam 5:1–5; 7:1).

So by the time we get to the first century, do we really expect the day of Messiah—the King of Kings and the Son of David—along with his messianic kingdom to arrive by anything short of a "wonder of wonders" and "miracle of miracles?"[15] Not a chance. Not when you're Jewish. The God of the Jews is the God of the impossible. This is the reputation he has been building all this time, in every generation of Israel's history, and he puts it on full display for the nations to behold and marvel.

Following closely in the pattern of Samuel, God ripples forth a similar forerunner and prophet to announce the coming of the Son of David, God's ultimate King and Messiah. And is it any surprise that this forerunner's birth would follow the same pattern that traces all the way back to Sarah, Rebekah, Rachel, and especially Hannah? As wondrous as a barren woman having a child will always be, it comes as no surprise to the Hebrew mind

---

14. "HaTikvah ('The Hope') Israel's National Anthem," The Goodman Camping Initiative for Modern Israel History.

15. Shout-out to one of the most beloved Jewish films of all time, *Fiddler on the Roof*. A must watch.

Chapter Abraham

that God should work in this way—alerting his people, getting their attention to yet another big, momentous thing he is about to do in their history, or a promise he's about to make good on.

And so like Hannah, the barren Elizabeth bears a son.[16] And the angel in Luke 1:36 revealing this good news about Elizabeth concludes with the words, "This is the sixth month with her who was called barren. *For nothing will be impossible with God.*" This conclusion echoes and answers the question God asked long ago: "Is anything too hard for the LORD?" (Gen 18:14). For Zechariah and Elizabeth, the angel's words sing a familiar chorus. Luke 1:65–66 continues to describe how everyone across the hill country of Judea was talking about this birth out of barrenness saying, "'What then will this child be?' For the hand of the Lord was with him." Of course everyone was talking about the Lord's hand in this turn of events because they knew every child in their heritage born out of barrenness was not only an important person but also signaled a momentous shift in Israel's history. God was going to move into and act upon another stage of his promises.

John the Baptist comes in the picture of Samuel, identifying God's chosen Messiah with the words "Behold, the Lamb of God, who takes away the sin of the world" (John 1:29) and anointing the Son of David and King of Kings with the waters of the Jordan (Matt 3:13–17).

Now, if you are impressed by an old and barren woman having a child, just wait until a *virgin* has a kid. What an even greater sign that will be. With this development within the ancient pattern, God heightens the mission impossible. It is far more impossible for a virgin womb to become pregnant than a barren womb, although both still require miraculous conception. Yet, a pregnant virgin is the sign God said he will give King Ahaz from the house of David to signal the big, pivotal, and prophetic coming of the promised offspring of David, Immanuel (Isa 7:13–14), who is King Jesus. In God's dare to King Ahaz—"Ask the LORD your God for a sign, whether in the deepest depths or in the highest heights" (Isa 7:11 NIV)—it is as though God were again echoing the same question from long ago, "Is anything too hard for the LORD?" (Gen 18:14).

Interestingly, it was Jesus who told Nicodemus the Pharisee, "Unless one is born again he cannot see the kingdom of God" (John 3:3). Isn't it curious that this was Jesus' response to Nicodemus' greeting, "Rabbi, we know that you are a teacher come from God, for no one can do these signs

---

16. This gets even more fascinating when you compare the striking similarities between the accounts of Hannah's and Elizabeth's births (1 Sam 1 and Luke 1).

that you do unless God is with him" (3:2)? As a learned Torah scholar, Nicodemus picked up on the miraculous movements of God through signs and wonders, as these were common in Israel's heritage and story. But isn't it also interesting how Jesus immediately directs and associates the conversation of general signs and wonders to the specific wonder of being born in association with the kingdom? "Very truly I tell you, no one can see the kingdom of God unless they are born again" (John 3:3 NIV). We can read this as saying it is utterly *impossible* to see God's kingdom unless you are born again. "Born again" is also imagery that communicates impossibility (as Nicodemus' response reveals). What is happening? Why does Jesus respond to Nicodemus with these words, this subject? He is, in short, taking Nicodemus all the way back to the beginning.

The theme of extraordinary and impossible births is, as we've seen, an ancient one tracing all the way back to the wonder of Israel's birth, God's set-apart kingdom people. The birth of the nation of Israel—beginning with Isaac's miraculous birth—points to the supernatural nature of entering God's kingdom and belonging to him. It's a mission impossible that only God can do by his Spirit, just as he has always done throughout Israel's history. The new beginnings God is birthing now through Jesus are in step with the miraculous beginnings that formed and followed Israel's story.

Also, it is in this conversation with Nicodemus that Jesus gives his famous words: "For God so loved the world, that He gave His only begotten Son, that whoever believes in Him shall not perish, but have eternal life" (John 3:16 NASB95). The picture of God as Father giving his only Son is not an isolated or random picture removed from Israel's story. The imagery and language of John 3:16 come to us in the ancient picture or ripple of Abraham, the first father of this great faith, offering on the altar his one and only son as a sacrifice (Gen 22:1–19)—the miraculous son begotten through divine promise and through whom the entire nation and kingdom of Israel would be supernaturally birthed. Just as Isaac was the promised door through which God's holy and kingdom people would be raised up, so Jesus is the promised door through which all people can enter into God's kingdom of priests and a holy nation via rebirth.

The ripple of being reborn continues in the New Testament and to this day, albeit now with even more development. The kingdom people of God are both Jews and gentiles who are reborn miraculously and supernaturally by God's Spirit through God's (miraculously) begotten Son.

Chapter Abraham

Before you move on to the next chapter, take some time to meditate on this ripple in *your* life:

1. Which of God's promises might your soul secretly laugh at because of how impossible or beyond nature it seems? Are there any promises you are forcing into existence by your own strength and reasoning through some practical "plan B"? Could it be that your struggle with that promise means that God wants to embark on something big and pivotal in *your* life?

2. Do you personally know the answer to the question "Is anything too difficult for the Lord?" Like Sarah, have you come to discover this answer for yourself?

3. How much does your view of the God of Israel align with the record we have on him—according to the reputation he has built, as the God of hope even against impossible odds?

4. And finally, are you out to build a reputable name for yourself, like the nations at Babel, or are you committed to building up God's name? Just like with Abraham and Sarah, he wants to build his glorious reputation in your life, too. How will you respond?

Chapter Joseph

STORY RIPPLE: THE GOOD NEWS OF RECONCILIATION

Like Abraham and Sarah, Joseph's story continues to testify and teach us about the God of hope against all odds. Joseph's entire life story is special in that it frames the gospel of reconciliation and foreshadows the Messiah. In other words, it is an early ripple setting into motion the gospel itself. Joseph's story also serves as a prophetic picture of events and promises that have not yet come to pass, even today. For these reasons, we are going to survey his story from beginning to end instead of looking at a few specific verses.

The key message in this patriarch's story, despite the rejection, suffering, and horrible odds, is that God is in total, formidable control, outwitting those very odds meant for evil and using them for profound good, abundant blessing, preservation of life, and lavish love. As we will see, all of these themes ripple into the very heart of Jesus and his gospel.

As soon as we meet Joseph, we notice he is a man constantly vacillating between favor and disfavor. This pattern will follow Joseph throughout most of his life. His experiences will be framed by great favor and equally great odds—repeatedly. Let's trace this pattern throughout his story.

During his upbringing, Joseph possesses special favor with his father, Jacob, and dangerous disfavor with his embittered brothers (Gen 37:3–4). The favor with his father is represented by the colorful coat Jacob gives only to Joseph (37:3). And when it comes to Joseph's prophetic visions and ability to interpret dreams (37:5–7, 19), we see Joseph again set apart from his other brothers by a bestowal of favor and gifting from God himself. This profile of unique favor already hints toward the unique and immense favor

Chapter Joseph

Jesus also possessed in the eyes of the Father. Not only did Jesus grow up having "favor with God and man" (Luke 2:52), but God sets Jesus uniquely apart from the rest of Israel saying, "This is my beloved Son, with whom I am well pleased" (Matt 3:17).

Despite Joseph's great favor (or because of it), great odds quickly stack against him. He soon gets rejected and sold by his jealous brothers as a slave (37:18–36). This is a major blow not only to such a promising and gifted individual but to a family member. The brothers, who are the future tribes and leaders of Israel, commit a grave sin and injustice against their own flesh and blood. Jesus, too, gets rejected by his own jealous kinsmen, the leaders of Israel, as well as his own disciple, Judas, who, in the same spirit of Joseph's brothers, literally sells him out for money (Gen 37:28; cf. Matt 26:3–5, 14–16).

Nevertheless, God is with Joseph in his captivity and makes him prosper in everything he does (Gen 39:3). Wherever Joseph went and whatever he did, blessings and favor pour forth on Joseph and those around him (39:5). This supernatural favor follows Jesus, too, and on a much larger scale. Jesus heals everyone who comes to him (Matt 12:15) and wins authoritative favor in the eyes of the people who hear him teach (Matt 7:29).

Despite his slavery, Joseph quickly gains the favor of his Egyptian master, Potiphar, who entrusts the care of his entire household to Joseph (39:4–6). Just when things begin to look up again for Joseph, disfavor strikes again. The same master who immensely favored Joseph soon rejects Joseph because of a false accusation on the part of Potiphar's wife and throws him in jail (Gen 39:7–23)—an even worse and stricter confinement than slavery. Similarly, after being sold out by his kinsmen and put in jail, Jesus also gains favor and even acquittal in the eyes of Pilate, the Roman governor, and his wife. Presiding over Jesus' trial, Pilate clearly says, "I find no guilt in him" (John 19:4), and his wife prophetically discerns Jesus to be a "righteous man," urging her husband to have nothing to do with him (Matt 27:19). But despite his righteousness and innocence, Jesus—like Joseph—suffers unjust punishment instead.

While in prison, Joseph comes across a chance to be released with the chief cupbearer whose dream Joseph interprets (Gen 40); but alas, the odds are against him—the guy forgets all about Joseph (40:23)! Disappointing disfavor also wins the day with Jesus despite his favor with Pilate. When an opportunity opens for Jesus to be released, the people cry out for Barnabas' freedom instead of Jesus'. Pilate caves in to the pressure and condemns Jesus to a far worse confinement than imprisonment—death on a cross (Luke 23:18–25). What really dampens both Joseph's and Jesus' situations is the fact that these difficult and deadly consequences come on the heels of their choice to obey God and hold fast to their integrity in the face of injustice. Despite their righteousness, the odds seem to prevail against Joseph and Jesus. At this depressive point, one might even be tempted to think that perhaps God himself was against Joseph and Jesus.

After *two more years* in prison (since interpreting the cupbearer's dream), God at last redeems the wasted years in Joseph's life by multiplying the favor and elevating his lowly status. Out of the darkness of dusty prison chains, the Lord raises Joseph to a new life as Pharaoh's right-hand man and second in command over all Egypt (Gen 41:39–41). He goes from prisoner to prime minister. Having been the only one in Egypt able to interpret Pharaoh's dream, Pharaoh himself says of Joseph, "Can we find a man like this, in whom is the Spirit of God?" (41:38). And in Jesus' case, after a brutal death and two days in a tomb, God raises him from the chains of death, thereby vindicating Jesus and his divine favor. God elevates Jesus' status from a cursed sin bearer to a victorious king who alone is worthy to sit and rule at the right hand of the Father (Rom 8:34). Like Joseph was given authority over Egypt, Jesus is granted *all* authority in heaven and on earth (Matt 28:18). Pharaoh's question actually applies to Jesus far more than it did to Joseph: "Can we find a man like this, in whom is the Spirit of God?" (Gen 41:38). Finally, with both Joseph and Jesus in power, salvation spreads to a famished world (Gen 41:57 cf. Matt 28:18–20).

But the favor doesn't stop there. As only God can do, the Lord turns the evils Joseph endured into a blessing for many. He reunites and reconciles Joseph with his brothers, Jacob, and the whole family again. And in that reconciliation, life is saved (Gen 50:20). I can imagine how, at that time, the odds of such a reunion happening—let alone reconciliation—probably seemed impossible from Joseph's perspective, from his brothers' perspective, and from Jacob's grief-stricken perspective. It is likely Joseph thought he would never see his family again, let alone have a chance to reconcile with them. But the fact that—against all the odds—reconciliation did happen proves God always had the *biggest* big picture in mind and worked miracles to make it happen. It is the same with Jesus, whose story is patterned upon Joseph's story. Even against the impossible odds of death, God's bigger purpose sovereignly and miraculously turned the greatest evil (Jesus' crucifixion) into the greatest reconciliation that saves lives forever.

Chapter Joseph

But it doesn't stop there. Joseph's story also serves as a prophetic pattern for both current and future events on an even larger messianic scale. Just as the brothers did not at first recognize Joseph as their brother but only regarded him as an Egyptian ruler over gentiles, so the majority of Jewish people to this day perceive Jesus as reigning over and belonging to primarily gentiles, not realizing he is one of them, their own brother—and their only help against the raging spiritual famine.[1] Indeed, many Jewish people do not even know Jesus was Jewish, let alone their Messiah.[2]

But just as the brothers beheld and bowed before Joseph whom they rejected and cast into the pit, one day, all Israel will bow and behold "him whom they have pierced" and "mourn for him, as one mourns for an only child" (Zech 12:10)—just as Jacob indeed mourned bitterly over the loss of his beloved child (Gen 37:34–35). Just as God caused the rejecting, jealous brothers to reconcile with Joseph, one day God will cause all Israel, who nationally rejects Jesus to this day, to reunite and reconcile with their brother and Messiah, Jesus.

Like Joseph saved all Israel in his day from famine and physical death, so Jesus will save "all Israel" (Rom 11:26) from spiritual famine and death. Genesis 41:57 says, "Every nation came to Joseph in Egypt to buy grain, for the famine was severe in every land" (HCSB). This picture is a ripple expanding toward future days (today!) when people from all tongues, tribes, and nations run to Jesus, the Bread of life, just as the whole world ran to Joseph for grain. And the great news is that one day Israel will be among them. Jesus' brothers and sisters will show up, too, reconciling and receiving the Bread of life. In this way "all Israel will be saved" (Rom 11:26). Those are some considerable odds, but the God of Israel is the God of hope against all odds.

Joseph's story is one of the earliest ways the Scripture frames God's lavish forgiveness *before* Jesus shows up and for *when* Jesus shows up. The forgiveness and reconciliation we see poured out on the cross in Jesus' story is a much larger ripple that developed out of Joseph's example. His life story sets off a messianic precedent of a lavish love pardoning unthinkable betrayal.

---

1. See similar connections between Joseph and Jesus in Hamilton, "Was Joseph a Type?," 68.

2. Chosen People Ministries, "Presenting Messiah." Some Jewish people believe Jesus converted to Christianity. Jewish believer Jonathan Bernis even recalls believing Jesus was born in Rome in the Vatican! One for Israel, "Jonathan Bernis," 7:05–7:15.

Like with Joseph, Jesus' own rejection, suffering, imprisonment, and separation from his Father preserves *our* life and blessing. He conquered all the odds—the worst of the world's odds—for our eternal benefit. Jesus, the greater Joseph, experienced and overcame the last and ultimate odds of sin, Satan, and death. And he defeated evil by the power Joseph himself tapped into: the forgiveness of sins. In the Bible, this is God's ultimate fight against the ultimate odds. "God shows his love for us in that while we were still sinners, Christ died for us" (Rom 5:8). While we were still weak, powerless, and without hope, "Christ died for the ungodly" (Rom 5:6). This is a hope that sees us at our worst, our most hopeless—when the odds are most against us. And it does not give us what we deserve, but instead loves us, forgives us, and dies for us in our place, exchanging our odds for his favor. Jesus fought and conquered the worst odds and our worst opposition, thus proving he is himself the God of hope against all odds.

Believe it or not, Joseph's sufferings are echoed and recycled in Isaiah 53. But I will save that for a few chapters later because there is another key messianic character we must first meet who will pick up the ripple of Joseph's story. Stay tuned.

Let's conclude with some meditation. Like we observed in Joseph's story, God doesn't waste the years in which the odds are (or feel) against us. He always has something bigger and unimaginable in mind. Friends, God is in the business of redeeming the wasted years the locusts have eaten (Joel 2:25). The God of Joseph is always in control of the odds and opposition in our lives. He fights for his people. He is for us. God is for us even when the world is against us, when circumstances and other people are against us. And even when he sets himself against us and humbles us, as in moments of pride or sin that invite God's opposition into our lives (Jas 4:6; Prov 16:18; Isa 63:10), he only resists to reap into our lives a reward eternal and incomparable. He fights for us to share in a glory imperishable—the very desire of our hearts, even if we cannot yet see it. But like Joseph, we will one day.

> For this light momentary affliction is preparing for us an eternal weight of glory beyond all comparison, as we look not to the things that are seen but to the things that are unseen. For the things that are seen are transient, but the things that are unseen are eternal. —2 Corinthians 4:17

Chapter Moses

TYPICALLY, WHEN BELIEVERS CONSIDER any comparison between Moses and Jesus, we tend to set up camp at the great exodus and Passover story. We often exhaust our focus on the deliverance out of Egypt and the Passover lamb, which are indeed excellent and core ripples applied to Jesus by the New Testament authors and characters themselves: "Behold, the Lamb of God, who takes away the sin of the world" cried John the Baptist (John 1:29), while Paul wrote, "Christ, our Passover lamb, has been sacrificed" (1 Cor 5:7). Undoubtedly, the deliverance Moses brings to Israel is the foundational picture of redemption for recognizing Jesus as the deliverer who redeems people from slavery to sin, the angel of eternal death, and Satan himself, a far harsher taskmaster.

But in this chapter, I want to consider how Jesus is like Moses himself (Deut 18:15) and how their life stories parallel. We will trace details and patterns beyond the Passover story that add overwhelming testimony to how Jesus reflects the unique profile of Moses, making him a Moses-like Messiah. Lastly, while Jesus is the prophet *like* Moses, we will also consider how he is *greater* than Moses.

MOSES AND MESSIAH PARALLELS

Because of the enormity of parallels and assortment of diverse stories, I begin this chapter with an overview chart put together by myself and my colleague Juan Corrales from Chosen People Ministries.[1] Use the Bible references to read the full stories corresponding to each parallel. You may even wish to study this chart and share it in your conversations with others. In the following sections of this chapter, I will elaborate on parallels

---

1. "Parallels Between Moses and Messiah," 5.

between Moses and Messiah in light of one specific theme and then proceed with story ripples.

Moses	Messiah (Jesus)
Moses survived the slaughtering of infant males at the hands of Pharaoh (Exod 1:15–22).	Messiah survived the slaughtering of infant males at the hands of Herod, who was targeting the newborn king he heard about (Matt 2:3–18).
Moses' parents hid him for three months after he was born because they saw he was no ordinary child (Exod 2:2; Heb 11:23).	Messiah's parents fled to Egypt to hide him from King Herod's search (Matt 2:13–15) because he was "King of the Jews" (Matt 2:2).
Moses stripped himself of the glories of Egypt and chose to identify and suffer alongside his people (Heb 11:24–26).	Messiah emptied himself of all the glories of heaven and chose to suffer to the point of death for his people (Phil 2:6–8).
Moses returned to his homeland after the death of Pharaoh, who was seeking his life (Exod 4:19).	Messiah returned with his parents to his homeland after the death of Herod, who was seeking his life (Matt 2:20).
Moses asked God for his name, and he replied, "*I am who I am*" (Exod 3:13–14).	Messiah claimed the title, "*I am*" (John 8:58).
Moses experienced forty years in the desert and trained as a shepherd before stepping into his role as Israel's deliverer (Exod 3:1; Acts 7:30).	Messiah was tested for forty days in the desert before stepping into his role as the Good Shepherd and Redeemer (Matt 4; John 10:11).
God sent Moses as a prophet to Israel (Deut 34:10).	God sent the Messiah as the ultimate prophet promised by Moses (Deut 18:15; John 20:21).
Moses appeared to the children of Israel as their long-awaited deliverer from slavery and Pharaoh (Exod 3:10).	Messiah appeared as God in the flesh as the long-awaited redeemer from slavery to sin and the rule of Satan (Acts 26:16–18).
God revealed himself to Moses in a unique way (Exod 6:2–3).	Messiah is the unique revelation of God (John 14:9; Col 1:15).
The first plague Moses unleashed turned the Nile waters into blood (Exod 7:14–22).	In his first miracle, Messiah turned water into wine (John 2:1–11).
God gave Moses signs and wonders to perform so Pharaoh and the Israelites would believe the Lord sent him (Exod 4:1–9, 7:8–17).	Messiah performed many signs and miracles so the people and their leaders would believe God, his Father, had sent him (John 3:2, 5:36, 10:37–38).

Chapter Moses

Through Moses, God judged the Egyptian gods (Exod 12:12).	Messiah confronted and cast out demonic powers, exhibiting authoritative judgment over them (Matt 8:28–34; Luke 11:20).
Moses initiated the sacrifice of a lamb during Passover (Exod 12).	Messiah offered himself as the ultimate Passover lamb (John 1:29; 1 Cor 5:7).
God parted the Sea of Reeds ("the Red Sea") through Moses (Exod 14:21–29).	By walking on water and calming the storm, Messiah demonstrated divine authority over the wind and waves (Mark 4:35–41; Prov 30:4).
Moses drew water for the people from the rock at Horeb (Exod 17:6).	Messiah offered living water to anyone who came to him (John 7:37–38).
Moses lifted up the bronze serpent in the wilderness so the Israelites would live when they looked upon it (Num 21:9).	Messiah must be lifted up, and whoever believes in him will have eternal life (John 3:14–15).
Through Moses, God gave and taught the Law on Mount Sinai (Exod 19–31).	Messiah taught and elevated the Law in his Sermon on the Mount (Matt 5–7).
Through Moses, God rained down manna and quail for the people to eat when there was no food (Exod 16).	Messiah multiplied a few loaves of bread and fish for crowds of five thousand and four thousand to eat (Matthew 14:13–21, 15:32–38).
Moses spoke to God in a uniquely intimate way, *"face to face, just as a man speaks to his friend"* (Exod 33:11).	Messiah and God spoke intimately to each other in a far more unique manner—as Father and Son (Matt 3:17; John 17).
Moses' face radiated with the bright glory of the Lord (Exod 34:29–35).	Messiah's face *"shone like the sun, and His garments became as white as light"* during his transfiguration (Matt 17:2).
Moses was willing for God to blot him out of his book (accursed) while interceding for Israel (Exod 32:30–33).	Messiah willingly became a curse for us (Deut 21:23) to redeem all people from the curse of the Law (Gal 3:13).
In his parting words, Moses commissioned Joshua to lead the people into possessing the land, assuring him the Lord will be with him (Deut 31:7–8).	In his parting words, Messiah commissioned his disciples to take the gospel to all the nations, assuring them he will be with them always, even to the end of the age (Matt 28:16–20).
Israel entered into the Mosaic covenant with God through Moses (Exod 24:8).	All people enter into the new covenant with God through Messiah (Luke 22:20).

Not only is there an abundance of parallels revealing Jesus to be like Moses, but we can already see how Jesus was greater than Moses, especially with examples like his elevation of the Law in his Sermon on the Mount and Jesus' authority to welcome not only Israel but all people from every nation into covenant relationship with God.

Chapter Moses

THEME: UNIQUE RELATIONSHIP AND APPEARANCE

God spoke to Moses and said to him, "I am the Lord [YHWH]. I appeared to Abraham, to Isaac, and to Jacob, as God Almighty [El Shaddai], but by my name the Lord [YHWH] I did not make myself known to them." —Exodus 6:2–3

Who has ascended to heaven and come down? Who has gathered the wind in His hands? Who has bound up the waters in His cloak? Who has established all the ends of the earth? What is His name, and what is the name of His Son— surely you know! —Proverbs 30:4

His eyes are like a flame of fire, and on his head are many diadems, and he has a name written that no one knows but himself. —Revelation 19:12

We know God appeared in remarkable ways to numerous people before Moses' day, and any of them would be spectacular to behold. Moreover, his appearance and historic relationship to the entire nation of Israel is quite unparalleled. But God's appearance to Moses stands out from them all, with perhaps the exception of God's walking with Adam and Eve in the garden before the fall.

What is unique about God's appearance to Moses is that the Lord revealed his personal name to Moses: YHWH.[2] God says he did not even give this fuller revelation to the first patriarchs, including Abraham (Exod 6:2–3). Moses did not know God through a mere title like everyone else before him, such as El Shaddai (God All-Sufficient or Almighty) or Adonai (Master/Lord). Moses knew God's personal name.

Revealing one's personal name is, well, quite personal. We know from Exod 33:11 that God communicated with Moses "face to face, as one speaks to a friend" (NIV). Friendship is personal. So in Moses, God appeared in a very special, deeper, and more personal way. And all Israel benefitted greatly from this deeply personal friendship, as Moses relayed everything God told him to the people through this personal relationship.

---

2. These letters represent the four Hebrew consonants for God's name, יהוה, often called the tetragrammaton and represented by either the all caps or small caps "Lord" in English translations of the Bible. I stick solely with the letters because nobody really knows how to pronounce God's name.

We also know that in Moses, God revealed himself as a deliverer. Immediately after revealing his personal name to Moses in the burning bush encounter of Exod 6, the LORD commissiones Moses to go and redeem his people. While God has many titles and should be known through them all, at the very heart of God's most personal identity is the beat of redemption. He ties redemption to his personal name. Therefore, to know God on a personal level is to experience his deliverance. And there is nothing like a personal encounter with his redemption that draws one nearest to knowing the heart of YHWH. In the book of Exodus, Moses is that unique deliverer who knew God's personal name and spoke to him face to face, heart to heart.

Just as God appeared to Moses in this unique and intimate way—revealing his personal name that not even the patriarchs knew—so God the Father uniquely stamps his personal name on Jesus the Messiah so that he reflects the image of the invisible God (Col 1:15)—perfectly! Like Moses, Jesus experiences an even more unique and greater face-to-face intimacy and oneness with God to the degree that if you see the Son, you are beholding the Father himself: "Whoever has seen me has seen the Father" (John 14:9). Talk about "like father, like son." Nobody else in all of history can dare say he or she came close to such intimacy with the Father or worthiness to bear his personal name—not even Moses. Jesus alone knows and bears God's sacred and personal name in a way that is far greater than Moses, which again, was already pretty great and unique.

Additionally, just like we see Israel benefitting from Moses' personal relationship with God, we behold all people—Jew and gentile alike—benefitting from Jesus' personal relationship and unique oneness with the Father. Jesus invites everyone into the personal friendship he experiences with God: "No longer do I call you servants . . . but I have called you friends, for all that I have heard from my Father I have made known to you" (John 15:15 NIV). While Moses also made God known to the people, Jesus makes God personal to the people. In Jesus, we are brought into God's innermost circle. While Moses alone experienced friendship with God, Jesus invites all his followers into this deeper and intimate union. "I made known to them your name, and I will continue to make it known, that the love with which you have loved me may be in them, and I in them" (John 17:26).

Like Moses, Jesus reveals to the people God's commands but also God's heart behind his laws (see the Sermon on the Mount in Matthew 5–7). Moreover, Jesus follows in the footsteps of Moses by interceding for people in their sin[3] but in a way that is far better and more permanent than Moses or any priest throughout Israel's history: "Because Jesus lives forever, he has a permanent priesthood. Therefore he is able to save completely those who come to God through him, because he always lives to intercede for them" (Heb 7:24–25 NIV).

Jesus also speaks with God in a way that parallels but also surpasses Moses' experience. We know that, after meeting with God, Moses' face radiated with the luminescent glory of the LORD so that he had to put on a veil for the people (Exod 34:29–35). In Matt 17:2, Jesus' face and garments not only shine with the same bright glory, but Jesus is *entirely transfigured* before his disciples.

Moses and Jesus appear to their people as unique deliverers advancing a new era and covenant for God's people. Just as Moses appeared to the people as their long-awaited deliverer from slavery and Pharaoh, so Messiah appeared in the incarnation as the long-awaited deliverer from slavery to sin, death, and the rule of Satan. Each deliverance inaugurated a new life under a new covenant.

Moreover, God gave Moses many signs, wonders, and miracles to perform as proof that the God of their fathers did in fact appear to and send Moses (Exod 4:1–9). It's similar in the New Testament texts. God backs up Jesus through miracles and many signs and wonders (John 2:11, 6:2, 20:30–31, 21:25–26). Curiously, just as Pharaoh, the leader of Egypt, said to Moses and Aaron, "Prove yourselves by working a miracle" (Exod 7:9), so the Jewish leaders demand of Jesus, "What sign can you show us to prove your authority to do these things?" (John 2:18 NIV). In truth, it is not a bad question, and in both Exodus and the gospels, God supplied both Moses and the Messiah with an abundance of signs and wonders. Jesus even urges the people to believe *because* of the works he does: "If I am not doing the works of my Father, then do not believe me; but if I do them, even though you do not believe me, believe the works, that you may know and understand that the Father is in me and I am in the Father" (John 10:37–38).

Many of Jesus' signs reflect those performed by Moses. Interestingly, the very first miracle Jesus performs distantly echoes the first plague Moses unleashed upon Egypt. I imagine every Jewish eye witnessing Jesus turning that water into wine (John 2:1–12) being instantly reminded of Moses turning the Nile waters into blood (Exod 7:20). In the Bible, the images of

---

3. Moses interceded for the people three times (Exod 32:30–32; Num 14:13–16; Num 21:7–9).

blood and wine are intimately connected. It was Jesus who at the Last Supper lifted up the wine cup saying, "This is my *blood* of the covenant poured out for the forgiveness of sins" (Matt 26:28). Also keep in mind that in Exod 15:22–25, Moses turns bitter, undrinkable water into drinkable sweet water, which also parallels Jesus' miracle of turning bland water into tasty wine—the finest (John 2:10)! In witnessing Jesus' first miracle, a Jewish mind well versed in Torah would instinctively recall God's wonders through Moses.

Next, the wind and waves obey the command of Moses and Jesus, proving that God sent and was with both men. When Messiah walks on water and demonstrates commanding authority over the wind and waves through the calming of storms (Matt 14:22–33, Mark 4:35–41), he reveals the same power of the God who parted the sea through Moses (Exod 14:16, 21–22). Exodus 14:31 says that after the people saw the Sea of Reeds (Red Sea) part, "The people *feared* . . . and *believed* in the LORD and in his servant Moses." Similarly, John 2:23 says, "Many *believed* in [Jesus'] name when they saw the signs that he was doing."[4] In Mark 4:41, after Jesus calms the storm, it says his disciples, "Were filled with *great fear* and said to one another, 'Who then is this, that even the wind and the sea obey him?'" The answer to that question—which I think was in fact roaming through the disciples' minds to varying degrees—is, "He is one like Moses, but even more."

The Bible is clear: there is only one who has authority over the wind and waves. As Prov 30:4 asks, "Who has ascended to heaven and come down? Who has gathered the *wind* in His hands? Who has bound up the *waters* in His cloak? Who has established all the ends of the earth? What is His *name*, and what is the name of *His Son*—surely you know!" Through these signs and wonders especially over nature, God testifies to and backs up his chosen servants, Moses and Jesus. But in doing so for the latter, God is validating him as one who not only comes in the profile of Moses but in fact exceeds him. Jesus appears not only as a Moses-like Messiah but as

---

4. As a somewhat humorous bonus, I will throw in another parallel arguing that Moses and Jesus had very similar disciples. Consider and compare the following two verses. The first is the people's despair just before Moses parts the waters, when they are stuck with a sea in front and Egyptians behind. "They said to Moses, 'Is it because there are no graves in Egypt that you have taken us away to die in the wilderness? What have you done to us in bringing us out of Egypt?'" (Exod 14:11). The second verse is the desperate complaint of the disciples to Jesus when they are on boat during a storm: "And they woke [Jesus] and said to him, 'Teacher, do you not care that we are perishing?'" (Mark 4:38). Moses and Jesus both then proceed with their miracle on the water, commenting on their people's fear and lack of faith (Exod 14:13–16; Mark 4:39–40).

the very Son of God. Rabbi Nicodemus picks up on this Mosaic witness of Jesus' works when he tells him, "No one could perform the signs you are doing if God were not with him" (John 3:2).

As unique deliverers, Moses and Jesus both bring about key turning points in history. Just as the people entered into the Mosaic covenant with God through Moses which would stage the rest of Israel's history in the Bible, all people can enter into the new covenant through Messiah, which also serves as a major turning point in history—one that has officially ushered us into the latter days.

Finally, just as Moses had the unique privilege of dispensing the laws of God on stone, Messiah is still writing the laws of God on stony hearts today: "I will put my law within them, and I will write it on their hearts" (Jer 31:33) and "I will remove the heart of stone from your flesh and give you a heart of flesh" (Ezek 36:26). So, you see, a prophet *like* but *greater* than Moses.

The Story Ripples of the Bible

STORY RIPPLE: A KEY GENTILE ENCOUNTER

Jethro, the priest of Midian, Moses' father-in-law, *heard of all that God had done* for Moses and for Israel his people, how the LORD had brought Israel out of Egypt. . . . Jethro, Moses' father-in-law, came with his sons and his wife to Moses in the wilderness where he was encamped at the mountain of God. . . . Then Moses told his father-in-law all that the LORD had done to Pharaoh and to the Egyptians for Israel's sake, all the hardship that had come upon them in the way, and how the LORD had delivered them. And Jethro rejoiced for all the good that the LORD had done to Israel, in that he had delivered them out of the hand of the Egyptians. Jethro said, *"Blessed be the LORD, who has delivered you out of the hand of the Egyptians and out of the hand of Pharaoh and has delivered the people from under the hand of the Egyptians. Now I know that the LORD is greater than all gods,* because in this affair they dealt arrogantly with the people." And Jethro, Moses' father-in-law, brought a burnt offering and sacrifices to God; and Aaron came with all the elders of Israel to eat bread with Moses' father-in-law before God. —Exodus 18:1, 5, 8–12

After Abram returned from defeating Kedorlaomer and the kings allied with him, the king of Sodom came out to meet him in the Valley of Shaveh (that is, the King's Valley). Then Melchizedek king of Salem brought out bread and wine. He was priest of God Most High, and he blessed Abram, saying, *"Blessed be Abram by God Most High, Creator of heaven and earth. And praise be to God Most High, who delivered your enemies into your hand."* Then Abram gave him a tenth of everything. —Genesis 14:17–20, NIV

I will make you as a light for the nations, that my salvation may reach to the end of the earth. —Isaiah 49:6

And nations shall come to your light, and kings to the brightness of your rising. —Isaiah 60:3

Out of the anguish of his soul he shall see and be satisfied; by his knowledge shall the righteous one, my servant, make many to be accounted righteous. —Isaiah 53:11

Once more Pilate came out and said to the Jews gathered there, "Look, I am

Chapter Moses

bringing him out to you to let you know that *I find no basis for a charge against him.*" —John 19:4, NIV

Moses' encounter with Jethro, a gentile, in Exod 18 is a story ripple echoing Gen 14:17–24, when Abraham (Abram) met with Melchizedek, also a gentile. Just as Melchizedek, the priest of Salem, came to Abraham bearing gifts as Abraham was returning from battle with Amraphel, so Jethro, the priest of Midian, comes out with Moses' wife and children as Moses returns from battle with the Amalekites (Exod 17:8–16),[5] and before that, the bigger battle with Pharaoh.

Still more similarities abound.

1. Melchizedek brought bread and wine, and Abraham tithed to him, giving him a tenth of everything (Gen 14:18–20). Jethro brings a burnt offering and other sacrifices and eats bread with Moses, Aaron, and all the elders of Israel (Exod 18:12). While both are priests, it is important to note that the idea of "priest" here was not restricted to a religious sense but encompassed the political leadership of a chief ruler over a certain region. Melchizedek ruled over Salem while Jethro governed Midian. We observe Jethro offering not only religious sacrifices but also leadership advice to Moses on the importance of delegation and boundaries (Exod 18:17–26). Moreover, in 2 Sam 8:18, David's sons are identified as "priests," which is often understood to mean chief officials or leaders rather than religious priests (cf. 1 Chr 18:17).[6]

2. More significantly, Melchizedek praised God for his rescue of Abraham from his enemies saying, "Blessed be Abram by God Most High, Possessor of heaven and earth; and blessed be God Most High, who has delivered your enemies into your hand!" (Gen 14:19–20). Jethro also hears about what God did for Moses/Israel in Egypt and praises God, too, saying "Blessed be the LORD, who has delivered you out of the hand of Pharaoh and has delivered the people from under the hand of the Egyptians" (Exod 18:1, 10). Jethro's praise, however, becomes different from Melchizedek's (who is identified as a priest belonging

---

5. Sailhamer, *Pentateuch as Narrative*, 280.
6. Baldwin, *1 and 2 Samuel*, 225.

to God Most High in Gen 14:18) when he says, "Now I know that the LORD is greater than all gods" (Exod 18:1).

Remember, while story ripples are meant as a flashback to a previous story, they also serve to foreshadow new, more developed ripples in the future that carry differences alongside the similarities. While there is one more key similarity, let's pause here to consider how this encounter between a key Israelite and a key gentile ruler prepares the stage for a few things in the biblical future:

1. God's intention to shine the light of redemption to all nations through the witness of his people, and

2. the context for the "righteous gentiles" throughout the Bible who hear and verbally accept the witness of the God of Israel.[7] Our text above shows Melchizedek heard about God's rescue of Abraham, and Jethro heard about the great rescue from Egypt. Both of these key gentiles verbally testify about it. The term "righteous gentile," however, can be misleading. Note that only Melchizedek is associated by the biblical text with righteousness (Heb 7:2 says his name in Hebrew means "king of righteousness") while no such association is made about Jethro. Therefore, the understanding here is about gentiles who rightly testify with their mouths the truth about the God of Israel, and not necessarily through personal religious observance. Later on, we do see the development of righteous gentiles like Ruth who go beyond confession to adopt the religion and get included within all Israel (Ruth 1:16). While the Bible doesn't mention Rahab's confession in Josh 2 as a personal faith commitment like Ruth's, Rahab's words bear much resemblance to Jethro's and Melchizedek's testimonies: "For we have heard how the LORD dried up the water of the Red Sea before you ... and what you did to the two kings of the Amorites.... And as soon as we heard it, our hearts melted ... for the LORD your God, he is God in the heavens above and on the earth beneath" (Josh 2:10–11).

3. Finally, these ripples pave a prophetic path for the Messiah—not a fuzzy, mysterious path, but a well-beaten Jewish path that can be easily recognized and should be anticipated because of the previous ripples.

---

7. In Sailhamer's words, "The purpose of these parallels appears to be to cast Jethro as another Melchizedek, the paradigm of the righteous Gentile." Sailhamer, *Pentateuch as Narrative*, 281.

Chapter Moses

We will soon see how the Messiah's story follows in the footsteps of these two key characters in Israel's history: Abraham and Moses.

Significantly, these two encounters with a non-Israelite ruler-priest took place just before the launching of a major covenant.[8] Abraham met with Melchizedek just before God established his covenant with Abraham in Gen 15, and Moses meets with Jethro just before the launching of the Mosaic covenant at Sinai (Exod 19). While the rest of Israel's Old Testament history is governed by the Mosaic covenant, it is not the last covenant to be discussed in the Hebrew Scriptures. The covenant that fulfills both the promises Abraham received and the laws Moses was given is the new covenant (Jer 31:31–34; Ezek 36:22–38), inaugurated by Jesus himself.

And what chief gentile ruler does Jesus encounter just prior to launching this new covenant? Pontius Pilate, the chief ruler over Jerusalem in Jesus' day. Of course, at first glance, one would hardly think to compare Pilate to Jethro or especially righteous Melchizedek; but remember, the biblical ripple of the "righteous gentile" is not focused on personal religious observance or even moral uprightness (which are not associated with Jethro either), but rather proclaiming true testimony about the God of Israel. In light of this emphasis, when we examine the details of Jesus' trial and meeting with Pilate, we sense the ripple effect from Abraham's and Moses' own encounters with the chief rulers of their day, albeit more developed.

What Pilate is doing in John 19 is examining and rightly testifying to the witness of Jesus. And when we consider the words and the testimony Pilate gives about Jesus, we observe parallels that fall in line especially with Jethro's confession about Moses' God. But first, let's dive into the details of the narrative:

1. While certainly not righteous himself, Pilate pronounces right judgments about Jesus by publicly confessing Jesus' innocence multiple times. "Look, I am bringing him out to you to let you know that I find no basis for a charge against him" (19:4 NIV).

2. Every time Pilate says something about Jesus even in irony or ignorance, he is uttering the truth: "'Here is your king,' Pilate said to the Jews.... 'Shall I crucify your king?'" (19:14–15 NIV). In a way, Pilate even publicly testifies to the truth about Jesus when writing "Jesus of Nazareth, the King of the Jews" on the notice that he nailed to Jesus' cross for all to see (19:19). Moreover, Pilate remains unmoved when

8. Sailhamer, *Pentateuch as Narrative*, 281.

the Jewish leaders urge him to take down the sign and rewrite "This man claimed to be king of the Jews." Pilate's only response is, "What I have written I have written" (19:21–22 NIV). One must wonder why Pilate seems to care so much about not giving the leaders what they want especially after giving them exactly what they wanted: Jesus' crucifixion (19:16).

3. At one point (after a personal conversation with Jesus that seems to shake Pilate [19:8–11]), Pilate attempts to free Jesus: "From then on, Pilate tried to set Jesus free" (19:12 NIV).

4. It is also worth noting that it is Pilate who grants Joseph of Arimathea permission to take Jesus' body afterward so that it could be treated according to the proper customs of a Jewish burial (19:38). This is, on Pilate's part, a righteous act of honoring the dead.

Despite Pilate's righteous testimony of Jesus, it must be said at this point that, of course, none of these verbal confessions or even good deeds on Pilate's part justifies or excuses his ultimate giving into the pressure to crucify Jesus. In fact, it is in this unrighteous act on Pilate's part that we see even clearer parallels to Exodus 18 and Genesis 14:

5. Just as Jethro "brought a burnt offering and sacrifices" (Exod 18:12) and Melchizedek "brought out bread and wine" (Gen 14:18)—symbols Jesus used to refer to his body and blood (Luke 22:19–20)—so, too, would Pilate bring about the sacrificial offering of the Lamb of God: "Finally Pilate handed him over to them to be crucified" (John 19:16 NIV).

It would seem that Jesus' encounter with Pilate, chief gentile ruler of Jerusalem, just before the launching of the new covenant era, is a story ripple that got its prophetic start in Abraham and Melchizedek and developed with Moses and Jethro. And just like Abraham's covenant and the Mosaic covenant served as a light unto the nations (Isa 49:6, 60:3) reaching *some* confessing gentiles, the new covenant witness of the Light of the World (John 8:12) would spread to *every* tongue, every nation, every people, making them righteous—even sinners as bad as Pilate.

This paradigm of righteous gentiles ultimately finds its fulfillment in the universal church, a large-scale multitude of people from every nation under the earth who have heard true testimony of what God has done for Israel throughout history and who, in one accord, echo Jethro's confession,

"Now I know that the Lord"—the God of Israel—"is greater than all gods." Lastly, this church, like Ruth, gets included into the olive tree of all Israel (Rom 11:17–24).

The Story Ripples of the Bible

STORY RIPPLE: BUILDING A DWELLING PLACE FOR GOD

> And let them make me a sanctuary, that I may dwell in their midst. Exactly as I show you concerning the pattern of the tabernacle, and of all its furniture, so you shall make it. —Exodus 25:8–9

> These are the records of the tabernacle, the tabernacle of the testimony, as they were recorded at the commandment of Moses... —Exodus 38:21

> But will God indeed dwell on the earth? Behold, heaven and the highest heaven cannot contain you; how much less this house that I have built! —1 Kings 8:27

> In the beginning was the Word, and the Word was with God, and the Word was God. He was in the beginning with God. All things were made through him, and without him was not anything made that was made. In him was life, and the life was the light of men.... And the Word became flesh and dwelt among us. —John 1:1–4, 14

If you enjoy studying all the nitty-gritty details in the Bible—like genealogies, geographic locations, the long list of laws for everything under the sun, and instructions for the tabernacle—then this is the story ripple for you. And if you're the person who regularly skips over all such detail, then this story ripple is especially for you!

While I often like to read what the Talmudic rabbis have written in their extrabiblical books such as the Talmud or the Midrash, it is not as often that I encounter striking agreement between what the rabbis have said and what Christian interpreters say about a given biblical text. This section features one such agreement. For believers in Jesus, this consensus also happens to be a story ripple about God's dwelling place, one that flows right into the New Testament where it finds fulfillment. The connections and parallels in this section make me so giddy that I can't help but share it so you can be giddy about it, too.

At the same time, you should know that working through such details in the Bible requires some extra focus, determination, and patience before reaping our giddy reward. But I hope you will find it a worthy venture, since every jot and tittle of Scripture finds its fulfillment in Jesus.

Chapter Moses

Both rabbinic and Christian thinkers agree that the construction of the tabernacle is a recounting of the creation story. Exodus 25–30 is full of parallels, patterns, and flashbacks to Gen 1–2. And Talmudic rabbis have compared the two in great detail—as have Christian commentators.[9]

Christian Bible scholar John H. Sailhamer points out that just as God created the heavens and the earth as the "arena" in which God was to dwell and fellowship with humankind, so the Israelites created the tabernacle for God's restored dwelling place with humankind: "Thus the account of Creation in Gen 1–2 and the building of the tabernacle in Exod 25–30 have several significant similarities."[10]

The Jewish sages and rabbis make a similar point in the *Midrash Tanchuma*:

> R. Jacob the son of Issi asked: Why does it say; *I love the habitation of Thy house, and the place where Thy glory dwelleth?* Because the Tabernacle is equal to the creation of the world itself. How is that so?[11]

And so they begin their detailed parallels:

1. "Concerning the first day, it is written: *In the beginning God created the heaven and the earth* (Gen. 1:1), and it is written elsewhere: *Who stretched out the heavens like a curtain* (Ps. 104:2), and concerning the Tabernacle it is written: *And thou shalt make curtains of goats' hair* (Exod. 26:7)."[12]

2. "About the second day of creation it states: *Let there be a firmament and divide between them....* About the tabernacle it is written: *And*

---

9. Sailhamer, *Pentateuch as Narrative*, 298–306. Sailhamer will be the main yet mighty Christian commentator whom I shall reference in this section. Please also note that the rabbis and Sailhamer tend to highlight different connections with only some details overlapping, as the following pages will show; but the overall connection between the design of the tabernacle and the creation story is strong.

10. Sailhamer, *Pentateuch as Narrative*, 298.

11. *Midrash Tanchuma* Pekudei 2:3. All italics and abbreviations for biblical books from this source are original.

12. *Midrash Tanchuma* Pekudei 2:3. On a side note, this comparison to a curtain invokes the image of a *chuppah*, a canopy used at Jewish weddings under which the bride and groom stand as they get married. Not only is it symbolic of the home the couple will share together, but it is a strong symbol of hospitality, reminiscent of Abraham's open-sided tent and his hospitality to the three angelic visitors (Gen 18:1–15) (see Diamant, "The Huppah," My Jewish Learning). The earth God created, then, is meant to be both hospitable for humankind's survival and for sharing a "home" with the Lord himself.

53

the veil shall divide between you (Exod. 26:33)."[13] So a veil would divide between a holy God in the heavens and sinful humans on earth.

3. "With regard to the third day it states: *Let the waters under the heavens be gathered* (Gen. 1:9). With reference to the Tabernacle it is written: *Thou shalt also make a laver of brass . . . and thou shalt put water therein* (Exod. 30:18)."[14]

4. "On the fourth day he created light, as is stated: *Let there be lights in the firmament of heaven* (Gen. 1:14), and concerning the Tabernacle it is said: *And thou shalt make a candlestick* [or lampstand] *of pure gold*" (Exod. 25:31).[15] Speaking about gold, Sailhamer explains that both the garden of Eden and the tabernacle contained pure gold (Gen 2:12; Exod 25:3) but also precious jewels (Gen 2:12; Exod 25:7).[16]

5. "On the fifth day He created birds, as it is said: *Let the waters swarm with swarms of living creatures, and let the fowl fly above the earth* (Gen. 1:20)." Concerning the Tabernacle, God "directed them to offer sacrifices of lambs and birds, and it says as well: *And the cherubim shall spread out their wings on high* (Exod. 25:20)."[17] Speaking of cherubim, it is also worth noting that both the garden of Eden and the tabernacle were guarded by cherubim (Gen 3:24; Exod 25:18).[18]

6. "On the sixth day he created man, as it is said: *And God created man in His own image, in the image of God He created him* (Gen. 1:27), and about the Tabernacle, it is written *A man who is a high priest who has been anointed to serve and to minister before God.*"[19] Basically, just as God appointed Adam and Eve to tend to the garden, God appointed a high priest to preside over the tabernacle duties. Sailhamer shows that just as male and female were made according to the image of God (Gen 1:26–27), the tabernacle was also made according to the pattern God showed Moses (Exod 25:9).[20]

---

13. *Midrash Tanchuma* Pekudei 2:3.
14. *Midrash Tanchuma* Pekudei 2:3.
15. *Midrash Tanchuma* Pekudei 2:3.
16. Sailhamer, *Pentateuch as Narrative*, 299.
17. *Midrash Tanchuma* Pekudei 2:3.
18. Sailhamer, *Pentateuch as Narrative*, 299.
19. *Midrash Tanchuma* Pekudei 2:3.
20. Sailhamer, *Pentateuch as Narrative*, 299.

Chapter Moses

7. Rabbinical tradition even associates the acacia wood used for the tabernacle with the trees in the garden of Eden.[21] The ark of the covenant, the mercy seat, and the table for the bread of the Presence were to be made out of acacia wood. These were at the *center* of the tabernacle, just like the Tree of Life was at the heart of the garden, "in the midst of the garden" (Gen 2:9). Exodus 25:21–22 says, "You shall put the mercy seat on the top of the ark, and in the ark you shall put the testimony that I shall give you. There I will meet with you" just like Adam once met and walked with God in the cool of the day.

8. The rabbis and Sailhamer both discuss the parallel of the last day of work. God finished and rested on the seventh day of Creation, consecrating it as holy and instituting the Sabbath. Numbers 7:1 states that when Moses finished setting up the Tabernacle, he "anointed and consecrated it."[22] Exodus 31:12–18 also reminds Israel of God's last instruction to observe the Lord's Sabbath upon completion of the tabernacle.[23] Moreover, in Genesis, God concludes his creation with an inspection and evaluation of all he had done: "God saw all he had made, and behold, it was very good" (Gen 1:31). And in Exod 39:42, "The Israelites had done all the work just as the Lord had commanded Moses." Although not stated plainly, doing the work of the Lord according to the exact will of the Lord is indeed very good. It is a reflection of God's goodness. In fact, this text is *repeated* in the very next verse: "Moses inspected the work and saw that they had done it just as the Lord had commanded" (Exod 39:43). Although neither the rabbis nor Sailhamer point this out, repeating back to back that something was done exactly as the Lord commanded is one way of not just saying but *showing* that it was not just good but *very good*. It was so good that the point had to be repeated. Lastly, just as the creation ends with blessing on the seventh day (Gen 2:3), so the completion of the tabernacle also ends in a blessing from Moses (Exod 39:43).[24]

9. The rabbis even draw a parallel between the creation and the tabernacle serving as God's court witness against Israel for when she breaks the covenant. Throughout the Scriptures, God says, "I call heaven and

---

21. Sperber, "Targum," 4:129.
22. *Midrash Tanchuma* Pekudei 2:3.
23. Sailhamer, *Pentateuch as Narrative*, 299.
24. *Midrash Tanchuma* Pekudei 2:3 and Sailhamer, *Pentateuch as Narrative*, 299.

earth to witness against you this day" (Deut 30:19). And so even as heaven and earth bear witness concerning Israel, "so the tabernacle bears witness on behalf of Israel when it says, *These are the accounts of the Tabernacle, even the Tabernacle of the testimony* (Exod. 38:21).”[25] So both creation and the tabernacle serve the function of holding God's people accountable and calling them to give account (testimony).

10. Lastly, just as the creation account is followed by the fall (Gen 3), God's instructions for the building of the tabernacle is also followed by a "fall narrative," the sin of the golden calf (Exod 32), as Sailhamer keenly points out.[26]

Sailhamer writes, "By depicting the Garden of Eden in conjunction with the tabernacle, the writer wants to show the purpose of the tabernacle as a return to the Garden of Eden."[27] But of course, the biblical ripple of God's dwelling places continues to develop from Eden, to the tabernacle, and to the temple, which retains the creation/tabernacle pattern but where King Solomon introduces a mysterious paradox: "Will God indeed dwell on the earth? Behold, heaven and the highest heaven cannot contain you; how much less this house that I have built!" (1 Kgs 8:27).

Will the Creator inhabit his own creation? How can the finite contain the infinite? How can God's invisible and omnipresent Spirit inhabit a visible, physical form? How can God's holy presence dwell among a man-made tent of decaying material goods? How can God dwell on the earth?

And yet he did. He walked with Adam and Eve in the garden, resided in human-made houses and temples, and later took on human flesh. "And the word became flesh and dwelt [tabernacled] among us" (John 1:14). While our English Bibles often use the word "dwelt" in this verse, the Greek root word here actually means "to pitch a tent,"[28] thereby rendering "tabernacled among us"[29] a better translation. In this one Greek word, our Jewish author and apostle John had in mind the tabernacle, the place of God's dwelling among the children of Israel throughout the wilderness wandering.

25. *Midrash Tanchuma* Pekudei 2:3
26. Sailhamer, *Pentateuch as Narrative*, 299.
27. Sailhamer, *Pentateuch as Narrative*, 300.
28. Bible Hub, "4637. skēnoō."
29. Only a few, lesser-known New Testament translations actually reflect the Greek by using the word "tabernacle" or "tent" for this verse: Anderson New Testament, Godbey New Testament, Haweis New Testament, Mace New Testament, and Worrell New Testament. See Bible Hub, "John 1:14."

Chapter Moses

God's own incarnation is the next climactic development in this ripple, and it is important to note that while God's dwelling in a body is a perplexing mystery, it is not unwarranted. The idea of the divine presence taking up residence in a body is no more mysterious and logic-defying than the idea of God's presence residing in a tent of wood, gold, and curtains. This was precisely the wonder of Solomon: How can any creation contain the Creator?

The perplexing paradox of God's dwelling place has been warranted by the Scriptures since the garden of Eden. How can the Creator inhabit his own creation and walk with Adam and Eve in the cool of the day? Will God indeed dwell on the earth? Will God abide in a house made by human hands? The incarnation is no more perplexing and no less warranted. These previous ripples have always been moving in this direction—toward a greater experience of God's presence.

Just as God inhabited his own created garden, just as the glory of his presence fell and filled the tabernacle and the temple, so "in [Jesus] the whole fullness of deity dwells bodily" (Col 2:9). That God saw it fit to dwell in a human body ought not to be a stumbling block; for, while the tabernacle and temple were crafted by human hands, the human body was created by the Lord himself, and for the ultimate experience of his relational presence. Therefore, Jesus is the perfect and better dwelling place of God.

John 1:4 states about Jesus that "in him was life"—think the Tree of Life in the garden—"and the life was the light of men"—think light from the lampstand in the tabernacle.

But the wonder of God's dwelling does not even stop there. Through Jesus, God's Spirit and presence will in fact tabernacle *within* fallen, broken men and women who themselves abide in Jesus. As believers, our bodies are now considered the temple of God's Holy Spirit (1 Cor 6:19). *We who are in Messiah are the next ripple for God's dwelling place.* We are the place of his preferred dwelling. And this is the vision of the new covenant, where God's presence resides no longer in an inanimate tabernacle or a temple but within his people—at last (Ezek 37:14)! And this vision ripples onward into the entire creation—the new heavens and new earth where God's Edenic presence can be restored (Rev 21–22).

Let us spend some time contemplating the meticulous detail and extensive effort invested into the tabernacle/temple so that we can have a relationship with God without being smitten by his holiness because of our sin. Let's meditate and take to heart just how much was required to reenter into God's presence since being banished from the garden. Consider what huge strides, what costly and bloody sacrifices God made to be with and within us again.

Chapter Moses

STORY RIPPLE: REDEMPTION RISES IN THE EAST

The LORD spoke to Moses and Aaron, saying, "The people of Israel shall camp each by his own standard, with the banners of their fathers' houses. They shall camp facing the tent of meeting on every side. Those to camp on the east side toward the sunrise shall be of the standard of the camp of Judah by their companies, the chief of the people of Judah being Nahshon the son of Amminadab, his company as listed being 74,600." —Numbers 2:1–4

Nevertheless, there will be no more gloom for those who were in distress. In the past he humbled the land of Zebulun and the land of Naphtali, but in the future he will honor Galilee of the nations, by the Way of the Sea, beyond the Jordan—
The people walking in darkness
have seen a great light;
on those living in the land of deep darkness
a light has dawned. —Isaiah 9:1–2, NIV

But for you who fear My name, the sun of righteousness will rise with healing in its wings; and you will go forth and frolic like calves from the stall.
—Malachi 4:2, NASB

Now after Jesus was born in Bethlehem of Judea in the days of Herod the king, behold magi from the east arrived in Jerusalem, saying, "Where is He who has been born King of the Jews? For we saw His star in the east and have come to worship Him." —Matthew 2:1–2, NASB

And very early on the first day of the week, when the sun had risen, they went to the tomb. —Mark 16:2

The traditional Hebrew title for the book of Numbers is *Bamidbar*, meaning "in the wilderness/desert," which is simply the Hebrew phrase taken from the opening line of the book. The English title "Numbers" came from the Septuagint (LXX) and the Latin Vulgate, based on the "numbering" or census of the people in the first chapters.[30]

---

30. Sailhamer, *Pentateuch as Narrative*, 369.

An important note about the book of Numbers is that it is not really an independent book. In fact, none of the five books of Moses (the Torah or Pentateuch) were intended to be read in the separated ways our Bibles today organize them. We must remember these "books" were originally scrolls, reminding us that the divisions are really a matter of sections that are part of a larger, unified work.[31] And it is critical to approach these sections of the Torah with a mindset oriented toward their relationship, connection, and unity rather than as stand-alone, independent works.

When we see and read the Torah in this holistic way, we are positioned to make better observations. As we study the structure of this larger work, one thing we are meant to notice is that the long list of laws (making up the entire book of Leviticus) is recorded between two narrative accounts.[32] In other words, these important laws are nestled between two key stories. The first story is the incident of the golden calf in Exod 32 and the second is Num 1–2, the taking of the census along with the orderly arrangement of the tribes in relation to the tabernacle.[33] As we pan out to view the sandwiching of laws between these two narratives, we are struck with the contrast that these two stories pose.

As Sailhamer points out, the golden calf incident is a picture of the people "running wild," but by the time we get to Numbers, we see the people facing the tent of meeting in an orderly arrangement.[34] One takeaway we are to receive from this structural contrast is that the Torah brings order.[35] The giving of the laws brought much needed order to a disorderly people. The laws that we see in Leviticus benefitted the people tremendously. They went from lawless false worship to orderly and organized worship of the one, true, and only God. They aligned with truth, in other words, and found peace. Truth leads to peace and freedom by ordering things in right relationship to God.

Next, let's pinpoint and explore two key observations from the orderly arrangement of the tribal camp itself, both found in Num 2:3.[36] There we see:

---

31. Sailhamer, *Pentateuch as Narrative*, 369.
32. Sailhamer, *Pentateuch as Narrative*, 370.
33. Sailhamer, *Pentateuch as Narrative*, 370.
34. Sailhamer, *Pentateuch as Narrative*, 370–71.
35. Sailhamer, *Pentateuch as Narrative*, 312, 370.
36. Sailhamer, *Pentateuch as Narrative*, 371.

1. the prominence and centrality of the tribe of Judah, who is mentioned first, and
2. the "east" and "sunrise" imagery.

1. The Rising Prominence of Judah

Within Israel's camp, each tribe was to be positioned facing the tent of meeting on every side—north, east, south, and west. There is great meaning to be found in this orderly arrangement of the tribes around the tabernacle, which, remember, represents God's presence. The first tribe to be mentioned in Numbers 2 is not Reuben who was the firstborn son (Gen 29:32), but rather Judah, which is quite purposeful. In Num 2:3, when God says to position the tribe of Judah "on the east side toward the sunrise," he is highlighting Judah's importance and centrality in the divine plan of redemption.[37]

We will get to the redemptive significance of this "eastward" position toward the sunrise, but first, let's briefly note that, according to the census that is taken, the tribe of Judah comes out to be the largest tribe with 74,600 men (Num 2:4). "As in Jacob's prophecy to his twelve sons (Ge 49:1–27), Judah has already gained the ascendancy over the other tribes."[38] Judah has become the ruling tribe through which the royal son would be born who would bring redemption to God's people[39] and obedience to the nations (Gen 49:10). From this, we understand the tribe of Judah to be messianic, the royal tribe destined to produce the Messiah who himself manifests the presence of God far better than an inanimate structure.

2. "The East" and Sunrise Imagery

In the Torah, redemption—or the hope for redemption—is often associated with the notion of "the east" and the sun rising in the east. The book of Genesis devotes a lot of attention to "the east."[40] However, it can be somewhat confusing because "the east" seems to serve as a directional reminder of both exile/rebellion *and* the return toward paradise and God's presence.

37. Sailhamer, *Pentateuch as Narrative*, 371.
38. Sailhamer, *Pentateuch as Narrative*, 371.
39. Sailhamer, *Pentateuch as Narrative*, 371.
40. Sailhamer, *Pentateuch as Narrative*, 371.

For example, in moving "away from the presence of the Lord," Cain settled in "Nod, *east* of Eden" (Gen 4:16). The Tower of Babel and Lot's journey toward Sodom are also associated with this eastward direction (Gen 11:2, 13:11). At the same time, the first mention of "the east" is when God planted "a garden in Eden, in the east" (Gen 2:8), and he established humankind there in the East, in the garden.[41] East of Eden would be the place where God would dwell and "walk" with humankind (Gen 3:8).

Although moving "eastward" is often linked to separation, exile, and judgment, "the hope is developed that God's redemption would come from the east and that this redemption would be a time of restoration of God's original blessing and gift of the land in Creation."[42] Sailhamer points out that when God said "Let there be light" (Gen 1:3), this "used imagery of the sunrise in the east as a figure of the future redemption."[43] Therefore, "it was not without purpose," Sailhamer continues, "that the arrangement of the tribes around the tabernacle should reflect the same imagery of hope and redemption."[44] Out of all the tribes, God placed Judah "on the east side toward the sunrise" (Num 2:3) because this redemptive return to Eden would come through the tribe and banner of Judah.

As we move from the Torah to the Prophets, this imagery of the sunrise in the east develops even further. In Mal 4, which includes a clear and prominent messianic prophecy where God says he will send Elijah before the day of the Lord, we read the following just before the mention of Elijah:

> But for you who fear My name, *the sun of righteousness will rise with healing in its wings*; and you will go forth and frolic like calves from the stall. And you will crush the wicked underfoot, for they will be ashes under the soles of your feet on the day that I am preparing," says the Lord of armies. (4:2–3, NASB)

Here, we more clearly see the pairing of God's redemption with the eastward rise of the sun. We also more clearly understand what that day of redemption will encompass: righteousness, healing, and the crushing of the wicked in justice. This prophetic passage is like Gandalf, the righteous white wizard, saying in *The Two Towers* film, "Look to my coming at first light. . . . At dawn, look to the east!"[45] In strange, syncopated rhythm with Mal

---

41. Sailhamer, *Pentateuch as Narrative*, 371.
42. Sailhamer, *Pentateuch as Narrative*, 371.
43. Sailhamer, *Pentateuch as Narrative*, 371.
44. Sailhamer, *Pentateuch as Narrative*, 371–372.
45. Jackson, *Two Towers*.

Chapter Moses

4:2–3, Gandalf's return quite literally crushes the wicked orcs underfoot, as he, Éomer, and two-thousand Rohirrim cavalry descend the mountain with the blinding brilliance of the sun's first light. Gandalf's words (in the movie, not the novel) do well to sum up the messianic expectation in the prophetic writings toward a coming day of redemption.

We should also note the verse that comes right after Mal 4:2–3: "Remember the Law of Moses My servant, the statutes and ordinances which I commanded him in Horeb for all Israel" (4:4). It is important to see that what follows the strong messianic prophecy in Mal 4:2–3 is a reference back to the Torah—to all the laws that brought order to Israel. It is a reference to the redemptive movement flowing out of the order the Law brought to the tribes of Israel. This is a good example of how the Bible continually remembers and alludes to the past even while prophetically foreshadowing the messianic future.

Finally, when we reach the first century, messianic expectations have developed even more, and the concepts of the east and the sunrise are not only preserved, not only further developed, but finally fulfilled. The Gospel of Matthew opens by saying, "Now after Jesus was born in Bethlehem of Judea in the days of Herod the king, magi arrived in Jerusalem, saying, 'Where is He who has been born King of the Jews? For we saw His *star in the east* and have come to worship Him'" (2:1–2). The Greek word for "east" (*anatolē*) in this text also means "rising" and is "used to describe the rising of celestial bodies, the direction of the east, and metaphorically, the coming of a significant figure or event."[46] This word originates from the Greek verb *anatellō*, meaning "to rise" or "to spring up," which is also often used in the context of the rising of the sun/celestial bodies but also the sprouting or growth of plants.[47]

The star of the promised ruler from the prominent tribe of Judah is itself positioned in the east, and moving toward its rising is how the Magi found the King of the Jews—the one to whom the scepter and the obedience of the nations belongs (Gen 49:10), who would heal us by his righteous wounds, and who would restore God's order, blessings, and Edenic presence back into our lives.

In Matt 4:13–16, Matthew explicitly identifies Jesus as that "light" dawning on the dark lands of Zebulun and Naphtali, the Galilee of the gentiles, which Isa 9:1–2 prophesied:

---

46. Bible Hub, "395. anatolē."
47. Bible Hub, "393. anatellō."

> Leaving Nazareth, [Jesus] went and lived in Capernaum, which was by the lake in the area of Zebulun and Naphtali—to fulfill what was said through the prophet Isaiah:
>
> "Land of Zebulun and land of Naphtali,
>   the Way of the Sea, beyond the Jordan,
>   Galilee of the Gentiles—
> the people living in darkness
>   have seen a great light;
> on those living in the land of the shadow of death
>   a light has dawned."

The light dawning upon the land of Zebulun and Naphtali (which were included in Galilee) was the light of hopeful redemption that would undo the darkness of exile and judgment. This darkness first entered Israel via these same lands—of Zebulun and Naphtali—when Assyria invaded and took those tribal territories back in 722 BCE (2 Kings 15:29).[48]

And the prophecy in Malachi about the sun of righteousness rising with healing in its wings takes on a whole new depth of meaning when we read the account of Jesus' resurrection in light of this ancient imagery of the sun rising in the east: "And very early on the first day of the week, *when the sun had risen* [the Greek root word for "risen" here is *still anatellō*], they went to the tomb" (Mark 16:2). And what did the women find?

Nothing! Or better yet, no *one*. For, "He has *risen*" (Mark 16:6)! Just like the sun rises in the east, the Son of God arose with the dawn on the third day, as the fulfillment of the Torah's hope of redemption rising in the east and restoring the paradise that was exiled long ago.[49] In Jesus, all the blessings of the original creation are regained. This was God's arrangement: his Son from the tribe of Judah would be at the center of the way back into God's presence. He is the way, the truth, and the life, and no one enters into the Father's presence apart from him (John 14:6). In this royal ruler from the tribe of Judah, we move out of the wilderness and into the promised land—a new earth (Rev 21:1).

As the sun dispels the darkness with its rising, so the Son dispels death with his rising. And one day, we in Messiah will also rise to everlasting life. But until then, as we wake up each new day with the eastward light of

---

48. Fausset, *Commentary*, 592–93.

49. Moreover, Jesus' resurrection is a fulfillment of the Torah's Feast of Firstfruits, where the first and best sheaf of grain was offered into the Temple and was accepted or approved by God. Besides the sun's rising, the sprouting or "rising" of a plant or crop captures the idea behind the Greek word *anatellō*.

the sun's rising, let us remember that his mercies are renewed for us every morning and that our hope in the Light of the World is surer than the rising of the sun.

THE EXODUS (RIPPLE) EFFECT: FROM ISRAEL'S DELIVERANCE TO YOUR REDEMPTION

The story of Israel's exodus out of Egypt is one of the Bible's largest ripple effects. After all, it is the Hebrew Bible's grandest picture of redemption. And it is interesting to see how later biblical writers and prophets take and recycle this original story, reapplying it to future generations and events as Israel's history develops. Tim Mackie does a wonderful job showing how, for example, prophets like Hosea and Jeremiah echo the original exodus story to frame the captivity that their own generation was experiencing as Assyria closed in on the northern kingdom of Israel (722 BCE) and Babylon ensnared the southern kingdom of Judah (586 BCE).[50]

In chapter 11, Hosea is, in Mackie's words, "poetically reflecting" on the exodus story, and God is calling Israel his "firstborn son" (Exod 4:22) when it says, "When Israel was a child, I loved him, and out of Egypt I called my son. But the more they were called, the more they went away from me" (Hos 11:1–2). And just a few verses later, Hosea writes, "Will they not return to Egypt and will not Assyria rule over them because they refuse to repent?" (11:5). This verse is not saying God's people in Hosea's day will literally return to Egypt; rather, Hosea is applying the ripple of the exodus story and its imagery to show how Assyria is now a new Egypt—another experience of captivity.

The prophet Jeremiah also does something similar in chapter 31.[51] He recycles the language, imagery, and story of the exodus to apply it to the most "traumatic and tragic event in Israel's story"[52] that took place within Jeremiah's lifetime—namely, Babylon's besiegement of Jerusalem. After burning the city and brutally killing many of God's people, Babylon then gathered and bound all the survivors just south of Jerusalem in a small city called Ramah and transported them as prisoners to Babylon.[53] So Jeremiah is remembering and intentionally echoing the story of the Hebrew children who were captured and put to the sword by Pharaoh in the original exodus story (Exod 1:22) when he writes,

> This is what the LORD says:
>
> "A voice is heard in Ramah,

---

50. Mackie, "God with Us," 14:25–32:18.
51. Mackie, "God with Us," 26:15–32:18.
52. Mackie, "God with Us," 26:30.
53. Mackie, "God with Us," 26:37–27:04.

Chapter Moses

> mourning and great weeping,
> Rachel weeping for her children
> and refusing to be comforted,
> because they are no more." (Jer 31:15)

To capture the grief, Jeremiah brings in the iconic matriarch, Rachel (wife of Jacob), who lived long before the exodus and Jeremiah's day. But he uses her motherly lament to poetically reach over the centuries into the future to yet another destruction of Israel's children—*her* offspring—who are again "no more."[54] Mackie very helpfully provides a modern example of the poetic equivalent: imagine the great Martha Washington, the first mother to the free citizens of the United States of America, weeping from her grave over the tragedy and loss of American lives on September 11, 2001.[55] The word of the LORD in Jeremiah is doing something similar: it poetically plays on the past to portray the present—and prophesy the future.

The gospel writer Matthew picks up on the exodus ripple within the Hos 11 and Jer 31 texts and reapplies it to another tragedy that happened in his day. At the same time, Matthew also senses the ripple effect of yet another, even bigger exodus story taking place in his day—of messianic proportions. Like Israel, Jesus is God's Son called out of Egypt (Matt 2:15), and his birth strikingly parallels the traumatic events of infanticide surrounding Moses' birth because of another power-hungry "pharaoh" named King Herod (Matt 2:16–18). However, this Son of God and new Moses will bring about another yet even greater exodus for his people enslaved to sin, death, and the harshest pharaoh of them all—Satan. As every Jewish poet and prophet in Israel's history has done, Matthew recycles and re-presents the exodus story in his day.

It is worth mentioning that all the restorations, redemptions, and returns Israel experiences throughout the Bible are developed ripples springing out of Israel's most iconic story of deliverance—the exodus. And even the exodus itself is a more developed ripple flowing out of God's initial call to Abram (Abraham) out of idolatrous bondage in Ur and into a new land of promise and a covenant representing familial belonging to Adonai (Gen 12:1–3). And even Abram's exodus out of Ur flows out of the original ripple of God's promise to return the offspring of Adam and Eve back into the garden paradise they lost—to redeem them from all the curses keeping

---

54. Mackie, "God with Us," 28:48–31:44.
55. Mackie, "God with Us," 31:59–32:13.

them from again walking with God in the cool of the day, blameless and without shame in his holy presence.

So when Jesus arrives, he's interested in a deliverance that is even greater than the exodus story and a covenant greater than the Mosaic law. Jesus is intent upon a deliverance that cancels the very curses wrought back in the garden: death as a result of sin and the serpent. "This is why the Son of God appeared: to destroy the works of the devil" (1 John 3:8). "I came that they may have life and have it abundantly" (John 10:10). "God so loved the world that he gave his one and only Son, that whoever believes in him shall not perish but have eternal life" (John 3:16).

So, in short, we observe how fulfilling the Prophets also fulfills the Torah. After all, what did the prophets have in mind? What Scriptures did they possess? The Torah, mainly! The prophets are working with ancient stories and patterns that they are recalling, retelling, and reframing in divinely inspired ways for their generation. Through them, God is divinely repackaging the past for another generation. The prophets are thinking in terms of story ripples, not psychic predictions that literally preview the future like a movie trailer before it happens.

Matthew did not incorporate the prophecies of Hosea and Jeremiah in his gospel because those prophets were enraptured in a direct vision of an enraged King Herod killing babies in pursuit of Jesus, prompting his parents to flee to Egypt. No, these prophecies are about ancient, attested patterns rather than trance-like states or even novel revelation that is isolated from the past. The Bible's flashbacks to the past also have a futuristic foreshadowing element to them. Like a ripple, you expect them to expand into the future—and can easily discern their pattern when they do. While prediction is part of prophecy, story ripples are the leading dynamic making up the nature of messianic prophecy.

The story of Jesus is not separated or isolated from Israel's story. By the time you get to the New Testament, "the train has not come off the tracks," as Mackie says.[56] I would add that the train hasn't even veered off onto a different track! The New Testament is not a separate book severed from the Jewish story. Actually, it picks up where the Old Testament leaves off. The New Testament is not new revelation coming out of nowhere; it is story ripples finding their fulfillment. It is stepping back and seeing the stroke of every story converge in a masterful portrait of the Messiah's face. And Jesus brings about this fulfillment by sharing into Israel's story from

---

56. Mackie, "God with Us," 20:15.

Chapter Moses

the past, especially as the representative Son of God, which is what these prophecies in Hosea and Jeremiah set the stage for. "Jesus is following in the pattern of Israel's history by entering into the place of his people's captivity and rebellion and emerging on the other side."[57]

The gospel is the greatest exodus story. Paul's vocabulary about the believer's new life, new creation, and freedom in Messiah is infused with exodus language. That is the story he is borrowing from—as did his ancestors. This iconic story is the cornerstone of the gospel. Therefore, for those united to the Messiah, Israel's exodus story becomes your story, too. In other words, the ripple continues—after Israel, after Jesus! Since the Lamb of God fulfilled this story through his death and resurrection, God has been weaving the patterns of this marvelous story of redemption in the real lives and experiences of real people, Jewish and gentile alike—such as the disciples, the three thousand souls on Pentecost, the centurion and his family, the early believers, the church fathers, people of every nation and language under every empire that has risen and fallen in history, and all the way down through the centuries.

In fact, the pilgrims who fled to the New World in the early seventeenth century had the great exodus deeply embedded in their worldview and even saw themselves as reliving this very story in their present circumstances:

> The Pilgrim fathers considered themselves as the children of Israel fleeing "Egypt" (England), crossing the "Red Sea" (the Atlantic Ocean), and emerging from this "Exodus" to their own "promised land" (New England).[58]

In other words, they shared in this ancient story. Their lives and futures were impacted and defined by this moving ripple from the ancient past. The birth of America with its unprecedented laws of life, liberty, and justice for all was sovereignly fueled by the ancient yet transcending spiritual power of the exodus story, whose ripple effect persists to this day, breaking chains of oppression and bringing more souls into true freedom.

Finally, it is the same, unchanging God who, after the Messiah's lamb-like sacrificial atonement, unleashed a new era of new life, a new heart, and a new creation under the law of grace. If you are one who has put your faith in this Moses-like Messiah and entered into the promised land of his

---

57. Tully, *Reading the Prophets*, 258.
58. Wilson, *Our Father Abraham*, 127.

kingdom flowing with the milk and honey of a new, free, and abundant life in the Spirit, please take a moment to quiet your thoughts and enter into the following spiritual exercise based on the Jewish concept of *zakhor*, which is simply Hebrew for "remember."

Spiritual Practice of Zakhor

Zakhor is the practice of actively recalling to mind the biblical story of the exodus/Passover so as to reconnect with it. We have seen on a theological level how the exodus story serves as one of the key biblical backdrops of Jesus' story and sacrifice. It is the very thing Jesus himself had in mind—how he made sense of his own identity as the Lamb of God and of his calling to take away the sins of the world, thereby sparing his people from the angel of eternal death.

But the point of remembering the great exodus story is not just for our minds to benefit from this rich theology; *zakhor* is meant to also stir up our own spiritual memory so that we *re-experience* the story today. And we can do this because—besides the exodus being the iconic backdrop to Israel's and Jesus' stories—it is also meant to serve as the spiritual template to our stories of salvation, our exodus from slavery to sin, the angel of eternal death, and the harsh taskmaster ruling this world, Satan.

So if you are in the Messiah, take a moment to quiet yourself and simply recall to mind your testimony, the story of your salvation. If you are able, go through the following exercise in a posture of slow, prayerful meditation.

> What were *you* in bondage to for so, so long? What cries and groanings did God hear from you? What sufferings did he know? For Exodus says the LORD not only *heard* their cries but he *knew* their sufferings (Exod 3:7).
>
> Besides Jesus himself, who was a Moses-like godsend in your life that came speaking truth, preaching the gospel, or even leading your journey to deliverance with power? Or perhaps faith seemed as foolish and absurd as putting lamb's blood on lintels and doorposts; nevertheless, you acted, you obeyed, you took a step into the light, you tasted and saw that the Lord was good indeed.
>
> What resistance or intimidating opposition did you face? Can you resonate with the Hebrew children's broken spirit, the depth of anger, hopelessness, and despair because of their cruel bondage?

Chapter Moses

Perhaps, like them, you too felt trapped with oppressors behind you and an ocean of impossibility in front.

And then suddenly, out of nowhere, against all the odds—and definitely not because of anything you did or anything within you—God split the sea for you and made a way through the impossible itself, as though going from death to a resurrected new life.

You look back, and you see that he even drowned your enemies who pursued and tormented you for so long; he did *not* let them gloat or rejoice over you (Ps 30:1). And with a cloud by day and fire by night, he brought you all the way to the other side, to a promised new life, to green pastures, to life more abundant, flowing with milk and honey. He gave you a mountaintop as high as the valley was low.

Do you remember that first joy rising with the morning, when he turned your bitter tears into dancing, when he loosed your sackcloth and clothed you with gladness (Ps 30:11)? And to this very day, you have favor for a lifetime—never again to return to Egypt. He transferred you into the kingdom of his beloved Son, to sit at *his* table and to dwell in the house of the Lord all the days of your life.

Hallelujah and Amen.

Chapter Israel

STORY RIPPLE: THE HOPE OF A NEW COVENANT

Then the cloud covered the tent of meeting, and the glory of the Lord filled the tabernacle. And Moses was not able to enter the tent of meeting because the cloud settled on it, and the glory of the Lord filled the tabernacle. Throughout all their journeys, whenever the cloud was taken up from over the tabernacle, the people of Israel would set out. But if the cloud was not taken up, then they did not set out till the day that it was taken up. For the cloud of the Lord was on the tabernacle by day, and fire was in it by night, in the sight of all the house of Israel throughout all their journeys. —Exodus 40:34–38

Behold, the days are coming, declares the Lord, when I will make a new covenant with the house of Israel and the house of Judah, not like the covenant that I made with their fathers on the day when I took them by the hand to bring them out of the land of Egypt, my covenant that they broke, though I was their husband, declares the Lord. For this is the covenant that I will make with the house of Israel after those days, declares the Lord: I will put my law within them, and I will write it on their hearts. And I will be their God, and they shall be my people. —Jeremiah 31:31–33

And afterward, I will pour out my Spirit on all people. Your sons and daughters will prophesy, your old men will dream dreams, your young men will see visions. Even on my servants, both men and women, I will pour out my Spirit in those days. —Joel 2:28–29, NIV

Chapter Israel

> But when the Helper comes, whom I will send to you from the Father, the Spirit of truth, who proceeds from the Father, he will bear witness about me.
> —John 15:26

> When the day of Pentecost arrived, they were all together in one place. And suddenly there came from heaven a sound like a mighty rushing wind, and it filled the entire house where they were sitting. And divided tongues as of fire appeared to them and rested on each one of them. And they were all filled with the Holy Spirit and began to speak in other tongues as the Spirit gave them utterance. —Acts 2:1–4

THERE ARE TWO KEY, contrasting events in Israel's story found in the book of Exodus. The first event makes up the climactic conflict of the story while the other serves as the resolution. Naturally, the resolution is found at the end of the book of Exodus when God's presence descends on the freshly-built tabernacle. Now, most readers today don't realize it, but this closure is huge. It is a huge sign of really good news.

Why is this conclusion so big and special to the book of Exodus? Because it is supposed to be read in contrast to another event in mind—one that is unfortunately really bad news. Do you remember what epic failure in the book of Exodus put everything in God and Israel's story in total jeopardy—including God's reputation in the great exodus out of Egypt?

The sin of the golden calf (Exod 32).

This sin was so grievous to God that he actually wanted to start afresh with another Abraham—Moses himself. In his wrath, God says he will destroy the people and raise up a new and greater nation out of Moses (Exod 32:10), which echoes God's actions in the past with the flood and creating a new humanity out of Noah. But in a new development to this recycled storyline and familiar punishment, Moses responds to God's wrath by interceding for Israel and reminds God that such a wipeout would completely jeopardize and nullify the redemption achieved back in Egypt—including the reputation God has purposefully built up to this point in the eyes of the nations who were already well-informed about God's mighty actions in Egypt (Num 14:13–23).

This is a gut-wrenching and heartbreaking point in the story, especially after such an above-and-beyond deliverance. As readers, we are supposed to be sitting on the edge of our seats, eyes wide, heart racing, sweat breaking out on our temples, and holding our breath at the suspense of Israel's dire situation. She has come so close to death; and in fact, she deserves it. She broke the covenant like an unfaithful spouse. The sin of the golden calf is a major disruption of God's plan and the main conflict of the story. But it is *not* its conclusion.

By the time we arrive at the end of the book of Exodus, we as the readers can finally breathe again because we see God not only preserving the people (like at Babel) but actually choosing to continue his presence in their midst, like a spouse who resolves to stay and rebuild the relationship with one who just cheated. We can even say God remarries Israel by redrafting another set of tablets to replace the first covenant that was broken (Exod 32:19). With the glory of the Lord filling the tabernacle in Exod 40:34, the book of Exodus closes with ceremonious conflict resolution. And we, as the readers, are supposed to feel quite satisfied because, despite this really bad news and a really close encounter with death, the story ends with good news. It ends with restoration.

This descent of God's presence in the tabernacle along with the earlier giving of the new, second set of tablets symbolizes the renewed hope of a new covenant, and not only for *current* Israel who would now continue to make her way into the promised land with the second set of tablets—but also for *future* Israel.

You see, these two major events contrasted in Exodus are prophetic glimpses foreshadowing the rest of Israel's future. The sin of the golden calf foresees and foreshadows Israel's continual breaking of the Mosaic covenant throughout biblical history. Israel's idolatry and covenant breaking would not stop in Exodus, unfortunately. She would continue to relive this sin through repeated falls into idolatry and apostasy, which we read about in the Prophets (Judg 2:11–15, Jer 2, Hos 8–14).

But the resolution of a renewed hope and a renewed covenant would *also* pursue Israel's future and define her story. Though God would punish Israel severely for her sins, he would also continue his faithfulness and presence with her, as is foreshadowed by God's presence filling the tabernacle at the close of the book of Exodus. Resolution and restoration will have the final word. The pattern of God's faithfulness to Israel gets its prophetic start in the Torah and ripples onward throughout the rest of God's history with his people. After every captivity and exile Israel experiences from the book of Judges to Malachi, God renews hope (and provides a new deliverance) for Israel again and again.

But we see the full development of this ripple of renewed hope and a new covenant (which would usher in the ultimate deliverance) in Jer 31 (and Ezek 37), where God promises,

> Behold the days are coming, declares the LORD, when I will make a new covenant with the house of Israel and the house of Judah, not like the covenant that I made with their forefathers on the day when I took them by the hand to bring them out of the land of Egypt, my covenant that they *broke*, though I was their husband. (Jer 31:31–32)

In just these few words, we hear echoes of Exodus when Israel first broke the covenant with their sin of the golden calf, and this breaking of the covenant was represented in Moses' literal breaking of the first set of stone tablets after seeing the calf and the people's revelry (Exod 32:19). But knowing this is not and never was the end of the story for Israel, Jeremiah continues, advancing an even greater resolution to the perpetual sin conflict:

> For this is the covenant that I will make with the house of Israel after those days, declares the LORD: I will put my law *within* them, and I will write it *on their hearts*. And I will be their God, and they shall be my people. . . . For I will forgive their iniquity, and I will remember their sin no more. (Jer 31:33, 34)

Friends, this is language of *presence*, thereby paralleling the closing event of the book of Exodus when God's presence gloriously descends on the tabernacle, even after such a ghastly sin. Jeremiah's new covenant is a more developed ripple flowing from the initial giving of a second set of tablets in Exodus. But in Jeremiah, God's presence will not descend simply *among* the people in a removed, distant object as we observe at the end of Exodus. God's presence will descend *within* his people; and instead of stone, his words and laws will be etched onto *their hearts*. This greater new covenant also will procure an even greater hope and reconciliation: the full forgiveness of sins. Such resolution will be accomplished by the glorious outpouring of God's Spirit—not only on a few anointed ones like Moses and Aaron but upon all of God's people. The prophet Joel also prophesied the same things, saying,

> And afterward, I will pour out my Spirit on all people. Your sons and daughters will prophesy, your old men will dream dreams,

your young men will see visions. Even on my servants, both men and women, I will pour out my Spirit in those days (Joel 2:28–29 NIV)

All of these story ripples get accomplished in Jesus, who inaugurates Jeremiah's new covenant into reality, unleashing God's Spirit to dwell, no longer in a tabernacle, no longer in a temple, but in hearts through faith. Jesus says in John 15:26, "But when the Helper comes, whom I will send to you from the Father, the Spirit of truth, who proceeds from the Father, he will bear witness about me." And we know Jesus did exactly this on the day of Pentecost in Acts 2, when the Holy Spirit first fell *within* the people. In Peter's great speech, he quotes Joel 2:28 as being fulfilled by the events in Acts 2:16–21.

Simply put, the biblical pattern we observe from the very beginning of Israel's history is that, even though sin threatens us with death and jeopardizes God's presence in our lives, there is hope even for the most grievous of sins. And we can be confident in this hope not only because Israel's entire history is patterned on it but also because we, like Israel, have an intercessor like and *better than* Moses.

Although God did relent from destroying the people because of the successful intercession of Moses (Exod 32:11–14), full atonement was not made, and people still perished (32:33–35). Moses' plea was not enough to secure total forgiveness, even though he offered himself to be blotted out of God's book (32:32). But when Jesus offered himself to become a curse for us all (Gal 3:13), his intercession "is able to save to the uttermost" (Heb 7:25), as his ministry is far more excellent (Heb 8:6).

Israel's and the whole world's sins are overcome and resolved by the successful intercession of this Moses-like Messiah, who achieved the greatest redemption and will make sure to close all of our stories in hope—hope for a renewed creation.

Chapter Israel

JESUS' DESERT TESTING PARALLELS ISRAEL'S WILDERNESS WANDERING

> Then Jesus was led up by the Spirit into the wilderness to be tempted by the devil. And after fasting forty days and forty nights, he was hungry. And the tempter came and said to him, "If you are the Son of God, command these stones to become loaves of bread." But he answered, "It is written, 'Man shall not live by bread alone, but by every word that comes from the mouth of God.'" Then the devil took him to the holy city and set him on the pinnacle of the temple and said to him, "If you are the Son of God, throw yourself down, for it is written, 'He will command his angels concerning you,' and 'On their hands they will bear you up, lest you strike your foot against a stone.'" Jesus said to him, "Again it is written, 'You shall not put the Lord your God to the test.'" Again, the devil took him to a very high mountain and showed him all the kingdoms of the world and their glory. And he said to him, "All these I will give you, if you will fall down and worship me." Then Jesus said to him, "Be gone, Satan! For it is written, 'You shall worship the Lord your God and him only shall you serve.'" Then the devil left him, and behold, angels came and were ministering to him. (Matt 4:1–11)

As I explained in the introduction, biblical writers use different literary strategies and genres to get across God's message. That is partly how we are meant to read Scripture—by picking up on these strategies and seeing the connections that the human authors and the divine author intended. We are not to fear the existence of such techniques in the Bible but learn to follow and unpack them well because it is in and through these literary devices that sound theology and helpful spiritual application reside.

God doesn't always *tell* us theological truths in the Bible; he also *shows* us. And he does this mostly through story/narrative. Grasping this reality is important especially when it comes to our ability to see and appreciate the "fulfillment" Jesus says he brings to the writings of Moses and the Prophets. We must train our mind's eye to notice the flashbacks, parallels, and connections to the Hebrew Scriptures that the gospel writers strategically weave into their writings. We are to understand them as precedents that set the expectations for the Messiah.

While all the gospel writers make connections to the Hebrew Scriptures, Matthew is unique because he is writing to a Jewish audience. As a result, he tells Jesus' story in parallel to Israel's story. This is a key strategy

Matthew implements to illustrate the messiahship of Jesus to his Jewish readers. In showing how Jesus shares in Israel's experiences, Matthew is building a strong Jewish case that Jesus is the Messiah—a Messiah whom Israel always expected and waited for. Moreover, in his gospel, Matthew outlines the very criteria his people ought to look for in their analysis of the true Messiah. First and foremost, he must share in the stories from long ago.

Back in chapter Moses of this book, we already glimpsed how Matthew records many of Jesus' life events in parallel to Moses so as to show his Jewish readers that Jesus is indeed that unique prophet like Moses (Deut 18:15–19). But when Matthew writes chapter 4—Jesus' desert testing—he is writing in direct parallel to Israel's wilderness wanderings.[1]

In reading Jesus' testing, our minds are immediately supposed to time travel back to the forty-year wandering when Israel was herself tested by God. In fact, Jesus' desert experience makes no sense outside of or isolated from Israel's own time in the desert. Surely, both Matthew and Jesus had this critical episode of Israel's story in their minds as one wrote about it and the other experienced it.

Additionally, it was the Spirit of God who intentionally drove Jesus into the wilderness to be tempted by the devil. The text clearly says "Jesus was led up *by the Spirit* into the wilderness to be tempted by the devil" (Matt 4:1). That intentionality is strategic, as is the rest of the account. It is full of connections, flashbacks, and rich theological truths bespeaking messianic fulfillment in Jesus; and it will be our job in this chapter to excavate much of that out.

Jesus' Story Is Israel's Story

In the Bible, the dry, hot, and barren desert is associated with trial, testing, and spiritual purification.[2] And sometimes, as in Israel's case, it is an experience of darkness, blindness, and rebellion (think the sons of Korah rebelling against Aaron and Moses [Num 16]). The desert wilderness is also a waterless place, which, in the New Testament, Jesus associates with

---

1. Please note I am not defining the wilderness wandering as officially and only beginning *after* Israel refuses to enter the land, but I am including the time Israel steps into the desert after leaving Egypt because, textually, we see Israel's testing begin upon her passing through the Red Sea.

2. "Desert."

unclean spirits (Matt 12:43)—spiritual oppression, in other words. Despite these gloomy realities, the wilderness is also a place the LORD takes his people, as is the case with Israel and Jesus. Yet, as we shall see, it is *never* without purpose.

Just as Israel passes through the waters of the Sea of Reeds (Red Sea) and then immediately undergoes a testing in the desert, Jesus too is driven by the Spirit into the desert immediately after being immersed in the waters of the Jordan River by John the Baptist. This is a significant parallel linked to sonship. God declares to Pharaoh in Exod 4, "Israel is my firstborn son, and I told you, 'Let my son go, so he may worship me'" (22–23). Also, in Hos 11:1, God says about *Israel*: "Out of Egypt I called My son." So Israel, as a nation, is called and understood to be the "son of God."

In Matthew, just after Jesus passes through the waters, God parts the heaven and declares, "This is My beloved Son, with whom I am well pleased" (Matt 3:17). This paramount declaration of sonship intentionally connects the Messiah and Israel—and intimately, too. Sonship is family! This connection between Jesus and Israel is an immensely important observation because it already unlocks some key theological truths:

1. Firstly, the Messiah walks in the footsteps of his people—even in their wilderness. He is destined to experience what they experienced. Their story is his story.

2. Secondly, we are meant to understand Jesus as not only the continuation of Israel's story but as the representative of Israel's story. He is the ultimate Son who will represent all the sons and daughters of Israel. Just as he unites himself to Israel by sharing in her experiences, he will bring Israel into his story so she can share in his successes. More on this shortly.

3. Thirdly, the biblical imagery of "passing through waters" becomes the major pattern and sign for becoming a son or daughter of God. From the days of the Torah to the gospels, this imagery ripples through time to believers today. Those united to Jesus follow in his footsteps by getting immersed in water as a public sign of their adoption into God's family, be it son or daughter.

Seeing Jesus' identification with Israel in Matt 3:17 is a cardinal connection. But what follows next is an equally important disconnection or departure. In the very same breath of verse 17, Matthew includes a significant addition to Jesus' sonship that we never hear in the Torah: "with whom I am well pleased."

Unfortunately, God is continually displeased with the generation coming out of Egypt, and Scripture not only records this displeasure but shows it vividly. More than once, God's anger burns so badly against the people that he wants to wipe out that generation and begin afresh with Moses (Exod 32:9).

This is a significant contrast that I believe the gospel writer wants his Jewish audience (and us) to see. In fact, every connection between what Israel experiences and what Jesus goes through in the desert is colored by this contrast. By connecting Israel and Jesus and then disconnecting them, Matthew is showing us that *Jesus succeeds where Israel failed*—at every point. But neither Jesus nor Matthew is doing this so as to gloat over or condemn Israel but to explain how her Messiah realistically executes the long-awaited redemption for Israel. Matthew is telling Israel how she can be redeemed by her victorious Messiah. This is not only good news but an ancient hope.

So now let's continue studying the parallels with this contrast in mind.

Parallel Temptations: Food, Forcing God's Hand, and False Worship

Not only do Israel and Jesus both experience a wilderness revolving around the number forty—symbolic of a period of testing, trial, or probation[3]—but even the temptations parallel one another.

First Temptation: Food

For the first test, the devil capitalizes on Jesus' hunger and tempts him with food—specifically to turn stones into bread. Interestingly, one of the earliest complaints Israel had against Moses and God right after leaving Egypt was for food.

While Exod 15 depicts the Israelites joyfully joining in the song of Moses and Miriam in celebration of their deliverance, the very next chapter hits you like a slap in the face. By verse 2, we see the same Israelites

---

3. Both wilderness experiences include the significant number forty (Israel, forty years; Jesus, forty days). In the Bible, the number forty appears in contexts of judgment or testing, thus signifying a period of trial or probation. See, Got Questions, "40 days in the Bible?"

grumbling against Moses and Aaron, quite dramatically saying, "If only we had died by the Lord's hand in Egypt! There we sat around pots of meat and ate all the food we wanted, but you have brought us out into this desert to starve this entire assembly to death" (Exod 16:2–3 NIV). Eventually, God sent manna. And when Israel got tired of the manna, they again complained about craving meat (Num 11:4–6). Unfortunately, Israel's complaints regarding food and water occur again and again throughout their wilderness wandering. In the Torah, Israel failed to trust God, demanding food and doubting God's provision for their survival.

In stark contrast, Jesus not only fasts during his forty-day desert testing, but he overcomes the temptation to satisfy his cravings by quoting Scripture: "Man shall not live by bread alone, but by every word that comes from the mouth of God" (Matt 4:4; Deut 8:3). Interestingly, the full reference in Deut 8 that Jesus partly quotes in Matt 4 is actually a lesson Moses gave to Israel saying God caused Israel to hunger and then fed them with manna in order to teach them that man does not live by bread but by every word of God. But Israel failed to learn to live on the word of God and crave it like bread, even more than bread. In contrast, Jesus refuses bread and feeds solely on the words of God for his survival in his wilderness. Therefore, the fulfillment of this verse in the Torah is found in Jesus' sonship.

Second Temptation: Forcing God's Hand

Perhaps the devil takes note of the fact that Jesus quotes Scripture; so for the second temptation he gets more cunning and ups his game. This time, he tries to use the very word of God to entrap Jesus. Taking Jesus to the top of the temple, the devil goads him to jump off by quoting Scripture, specifically Ps 91:11–12, which says, "For he will command his angels concerning you to guard you in all your ways; they will lift you up in their hands, so that you will not strike your foot against a stone."

The devil is tempting Jesus to put God to the test. One article says, "Essentially, the devil was telling Jesus to 'prove' God's Word was true by forcing God's hand—if Jesus was in peril, God would *have* to save Him."[4] Honestly, the devil is probably relishing in his past successes with this temptation and thinking, "Oh I got Israel with this one back in their wilderness." But Jesus' response is, "It is also written: 'Do not put the Lord your God to the test'" (Matt 4:7 NIV). And if we again look at the whole verse Jesus quotes from

4. Got Questions, "What Does It Mean?"

Deut 6:16, it tells us exactly *where* Israel tested God: "Do not put the Lord your God to the test as you did at Massah" (NIV). Massah, which means testing, took place in Exod 17.

There, we see Israel had arrived and camped at a place called Rephidim, but there was no water to be found. This caused the people to quarrel with Moses, demanding that he give them water to drink. Moses' reply identifies the issue: "Why do you test the Lord?" (17:2). The passage ends saying, "And [Moses] called the name of the place Massah . . . because *they tested the Lord* by saying, 'Is the Lord among us or not?'" (Exod 17:7).

At Massah, Israel was tempted to force God's hand and coerce him into proving his word, specifically his promise to take care of Israel and be among them. Unfortunately, the Torah records that the people continually put God to the test, even though God's promise to take care of all their needs extended to the point of not letting their sandals wear out (Deut 29:5) or their feet to swell (Deut 8:4). The mention of sandals and feet is a very localized and detailed point, similar to the striking of one's foot against a stone in Ps 91:12. It signals God's concern and thorough provision for every need, big and small. But despite such assurance from the God who worked wonders in Egypt for their deliverance, the people did not believe or trust. Instead, they put God and his word to the test so much that Deut 9:7 records, "From the day you came out of the land of Egypt until you came to this place, you have been rebellious against the Lord."

Thankfully, in Matt 4, Jesus succeeds at every point where Israel had repeatedly failed. For forty days of scorching heat, an empty stomach, and dizzying dehydration, Jesus does not give into the same temptation to coerce God or put his word to the test, even for his survival. Instead, he does what Israel could not do—he trusts God in both the big things, like his hunger and thirst, and in the smaller details, his sandals and feet. Jesus doesn't need to prove his sonship (Matt 4:3) to the devil because he doesn't distrust God's promises and thorough provision. Moreover, Jesus recognizes the devil's mistreatment of Scripture when he pins a divine promise (Ps 91:11–12) against a divine command (Deut 6:16)—a command which of course the devil conveniently left out in his second temptation.

What Jesus accomplishes in Matthew 4 is extraordinary victory in all the places Israel failed so miserably. He gains remarkable spiritual credit exactly where Israel indebted and discredited themselves, especially as God's son. In Matt 4, Jesus is connected to the same temptation but radically disconnected from the outcome. As the Son of God, Jesus identifies with

CHAPTER ISRAEL

Israel's weaknesses by walking in their dusty footsteps and reliving their same trials. And he not only does what Israel could not do themselves, but he does it all *for* them. Jesus redeems their failures through his successes.

Third Temptation: False Worship

Finally, for the third temptation the devil takes Jesus up a mountain (an important image to bear in mind) and tempts him with all the glories of the kingdoms of the earth—and then cuts a deal. "All these I will give you, if you will fall down and worship me" (Matt 4:9).

Let's get one thing straight: the temptation here is *not* the second part of the text but the first. You see, it is Jesus' destiny to obtain all the kingdoms of this world along with all their glory. This is the Son's inheritance, promised by the Father: "Ask of me, and I will make the nations your heritage, and the ends of the earth your possession" (Ps 2:8). The government will be on his shoulders (Isa 9:6). He will be given all authority in heaven and earth (Matt 28:18), and to him every knee will bow and every tongue swear allegiance (Isa 45:23; Phil 2:10–11).

So, the temptation in this bribe is for Jesus to seize his inheritance instantly and easily through a moment of illegitimate and idolatrous means—false worship. Now, we see the act of bowing down in many other biblical stories, and their meanings range anywhere from showing honor (Gen 42:6, 1 Kgs 2:19), paying homage (2 Sam 9:6, 1 Kgs 1:31), to expressing worship (Exod 34:8, Dan 3:4–5). In Jesus' case, it is for the latter. And we know this not only because of the devil's blatantly blasphemous words "bow down and worship me" (4:9) but also because this entire scenario should have already triggered in our minds the scandalous story of when Israel infamously gave into false worship in the desert.

The sin of the golden calf in Exod 32 also took place by a mountain—a very significant one: Sinai (Exod 31:18). The text says Moses was up on the mountain (for forty days) to meet with God while Aaron and the people waited at the foot of the mountain (Exod 24:12–18; 32:1). Up on this renown mountain, we have a picture of Moses essentially worshiping God and receiving holy revelation while the people are engaged in the exact opposite: idol worship accompanied by indulgent revelry (Exod 32:5–6).

So, in reading how the devil takes Jesus, the greater Moses and God's Son, up a mountain for this temptation of false worship, we are witnessing a twisted, counterfeit reenactment and flashback to this scarlet sin in Israel's history that is surely intended by the devil as triumphant gloating in Jesus' face. Exodus 32 is a picture of one of the worst sins in Israel's history (and by extension, the worst of humanity). But as we shall see, Jesus deals with the depth of this sin, too—redemptively and triumphantly. Thank the Lord! This is not only good news for Israel but a relief for us all, as God's grace abounds to the worst of our sins (Rom 5:20).

Now, what exactly was the temptation in Exod 32? Why did Israel build a golden calf, bow down to it, and even sacrifice to it saying, "This is your god, Israel, who brought you up from the land of Egypt" (Exod 32:4, 8 NASB)? While the text doesn't explicitly say, I believe there's enough historical and textual evidence to deduce that the people were tempted by the glories of Egypt they left behind.

Regardless of which of the two popular dates scholars place the exodus event—whether the fifteenth or thirteenth century BCE[5]—ancient Egypt was a wealthy and powerful nation. In fact, the period known as the "New Kingdom" (between the sixteenth–eleventh centuries BCE) is when the Egyptian Empire "reached its height of wealth, international prestige, and military might."[6] This is the Egypt the people of Israel are nostalgically bemoaning in Num 11:4–6 as they remember how good they had it back in the land of their bondage. By Num 14:3–4, the people are already proposing to return to Egypt because, even as slaves, they had meat to eat and other luxuries that this wilderness and this God of Moses didn't seem to offer!

Where I think it gets even more interesting is why they demand to build specifically a calf and why they say, "This is your god," even though the God of Israel was so powerfully and obviously in their midst. One of ancient Egypt's most popular deities was a cow-headed goddess known as Hathor, who was considered important in every area of life and death.[7] She was the "primordial Mother Goddess" who ruled over the sky, agriculture, fertility, and childbirth and was also associated with joy, music, love, dancing, and drunkenness.[8] Besides being the goddess behind Egypt's abundance and luxuries, she was also considered "the patroness of foreign parts and of many minerals won from the desert."[9] In God's judgment on all the

---

5. "Exodus: Fact or Fiction?"
6. Mark, "Egyptian Empire."
7. Ancient Egypt Online, "Hathor."
8. Mark, "Hathor."
9. Britannica, "Hathor."

gods of Egypt (Exod 12:12), I believe Hathor was generally the target of the fifth plague, the disease on livestock or cattle. It was "off with her head!"[10]

I mention this religious context to suggest that the worship of the golden calf wasn't as random and mindless as we often assume when reading about it. While sin is always foolish, we modern readers often look back with incredulous exasperation at ancient Israel's shortcomings and judge her for being tempted to commit such a primitive, grotesque sin for absolutely no reason. But it is only confusing to us because we aren't thinking realistically according to their context. We judge an ancient culture according to our modern values and worldview. But we must understand Israel wasn't tempted by something that was unintelligent, ugly, and undesirable. Temptation doesn't work like that. There were calculated reasons and perceived benefits, albeit false, that tempted Israel to build a golden calf. Like Jesus in Matt 4, Israel was tempted with a bribe. And as modern readers, we need to walk a fine line between never excusing sin while also properly orienting our judgments of Israel's sin according to the historic and cultural context of her day, not ours.

In the polytheistic world in which the ancient Hebrews were immersed—especially after residing four hundred years (Gen 15:13) in a nation that held the largest and most complex pantheon of gods[11]—the tendency to syncretize the gods was not only a temptation but a tradition. While syncretism is defined as the combining of different forms of beliefs and practices,[12] for ancient Egyptian religion, syncretism was a special merging of two or more names of gods to form a composite identity.[13] While scholars have drawn on many comparisons to the ancient Near Eastern understanding of the divine to make sense of this episode in Exod 32 (and even sanitize the "sin" component), I believe we glimpse an example of the Israelites' struggle with syncretism, most likely between Hathor and YHWH, in the scene of the golden calf. One of the key and earliest scholars who suggested Hathor (or Hat-Hor) as the inspiration behind the golden calf was Israeli geographical historian Zvi Ilan. He stated that Hat-Hor could be seen as a golden calf in many places in Egypt and countered other scholarly associations to the bull deity Apis by proposing the location of

---

10. A reference to Carroll's *Alice's Adventures in Wonderland*.
11. Britannica, "11 Egyptian Gods."
12. Merriam-Webster, "Syncretism."
13. Britannica, "Gods."

Mount Sinai at Serabit el-Khadim, where the cave or temple of Hat-Hor already existed as part of Egyptian worship.[14]

Even in their saying of the golden calf, "These are your gods, O Israel, who brought you up from the land of Egypt" (Exod 32:4), scholars have argued that the Israelites believed they were worshiping YHWH, especially as Aaron follows this declaration with a festival dedicated to YHWH (32:5), the God who *did* bring them out of Egypt.[15] The declaration is still tricky because, while *elohim* means "gods," it also refers to YHWH singularly (as an abstract plural).[16] But the fact that there is *any* association between the calf and YHWH in this declaration and in the events of Exod 32 makes a strong case for syncretism. Regardless of whether the Israelites' perceived the calf as a representation of the divine form, a symbol of the deity's attributes, or a pedestal/throne for the deity,[17] they all amount to idolatry. And every form and degree of idolatry is false worship.

I believe the golden calf incident not only suggests the Israelites' syncretistic practice of worshiping YHWH through Egyptian cultural symbols but also their attempt to amalgamate the God of Israel with the goddess Hathor, perhaps in desperate hopes that this ritual would serve as sufficient appeasement to guarantee the same kind of provisions and luxuries they experienced back in Egypt. The image of a calf, the desert, and especially the revelry are all strong connections to Hathor.[18]

In the sin of the golden calf, I believe the people were thinking God operates in ways similar to false gods—where you can force what you want out of him if you go through the right appeal. I also think God was working hard in that wilderness to *disassociate* himself in the people's eyes from all the Egyptian gods and idols they would have been familiar with so that they would eventually get the message: *ein kamocha baelohim, Adonai*—"There is none like you among the gods, O LORD" (the exact words are from Ps 86:8, but this message traces all the way back to Exod 8:10; 9:14; 15:11; and Deut 4:35).

Alas, the familiar saying is true: "It took one day to get the Hebrews out of Egypt; it took forty years to get Egypt out of the Hebrews."[19] We

---

14. Pill, "Ten Commandments."
15. Coogan, *Old Testament*, 138–40. See also Amzallag, "Beyond Idolatry," 208.
16. Hundley, "Golden Calf," 566.
17. Hundley, "Golden Calf," 560–61.
18. Eames, "Evidence for Worship."
19. The exact origin of this saying is unknown.

can identify with this complex tension today because Israel's struggle with Egypt is akin to the believer's struggle with the sinful flesh and old patterns of thinking. Jesus certainly and wonderfully delivered us from our bondage to sin, yet it remains a long and grueling process to crucify the flesh daily, even as God's people. And so, there is no ground for either anachronistic or patronizing judgments of the ancient Israelites.

In Matt 4, we observe Jesus refusing the devil's bargain that had previously worked on Israel. The devil had tempted Israel to think that through a moment of compromise and illegitimate means, they could seize the glories and abundance they desired that in fact were awaiting them in the promised land, a good land flowing with milk and honey—glories God had already destined to be Israel's inheritance (see Deut 6:10–12). In contrast, Jesus, who certainly longs to obtain the glories of his inheritance, chooses to go about it God's way, which is not instant, easy, or transactional. God's way may be prolonged, difficult, and even dangerous, but it is also honorable, relational, holy, and eternally rewarding. In overcoming the devil's last temptation, Jesus redeems Israel from the unholiness of her worst sins.

Literary Parallels as Theological Teachings

Very important theology resides in the literary devices of God's word. The literary parallels of these three key temptations in Jesus' and Israel's stories are meant to show and teach us profound theological truths.

Identify

Firstly, these parallels teach that the Son of God shares in the sufferings of his people. As Jesus walked in the dusty footsteps of his chosen people (God's firstborn son), the Son of God chooses to tread the wilderness of every one of God's sons and daughters in every age, including yours. He has so united himself to his beloved people that he experiences everything she does, every sorrow and every smile. Jesus identifies and sympathizes with you—in every temptation. Heb 4:15 describes Jesus as being "tested in every way as we are, yet without sin" (HCSB). I find that believers are quick to focus on and discuss the "without sin" part of this verse but far less eager to swallow the equally important reality of "tested in every way as we are." We don't really want to go there, do we? But at what cost? A Messiah who feels distant and unsympathetic to us?

But we can go there—we *must* go there because Jesus went there, into our heart of darkness and worst wilderness, without hesitation. And we can also receive the truth of his ability to identify with us without compromising. Jesus was not only "without sin," but the writer goes out of his way to show us how impeccable Jesus was in the face of temptation and testing—fully pleasing to God and in major contrast to Israel. He is sinless *and* overwhelmingly successful—on our behalf!

Scripture not only tells us that Jesus sympathizes with our weaknesses (Heb 4:15) but also shows us through literary parallels how Jesus identified with his people in all points. And we are to find comfort and encouragement in that because he does the same for us.

In Acts 9, we are told that Saul began to persecute the church violently, entering house after house, town after town, to imprison believers, men and women both (1–2). Yet, when Saul encountered Jesus on the famous road to Damascus, notice what Jesus asked him, "Saul, Saul, why are you persecuting *me*?" (9:4). Why does Jesus say "me," when the text clearly says Saul was persecuting believers? Besides the fact that Paul's main problem was in fact Jesus, whom he perceived to be a false messiah, I think Jesus' question also happens to be a rich theological insight into the believer's union in Messiah. Jesus has so knit himself to his people and his people to himself that there is a mysterious sharing of experiences. What we go through, he knows and feels it himself, in his own body. And we, in turn, are called members of his body, destined to walk in his footsteps and partake of both his sufferings and glory (1 Pet 4:13). The extent of Jesus' sympathy is an excellent measure of his love and nearness—to Israel first and equally to the nations.

Don't avoid drawing near to such a Messiah who has drawn so near to you. Meditate upon these verses and stories packed with rich theology about Messiah's sympathy, especially in your time of suffering, trial, and temptation. Don't risk a distant Messiah when he has gone above and beyond in showing the length he chooses to sympathize with us—even unto death. This is the wonder of wonders of the God of Israel and Israel's Messiah—namely, that he chooses to suffer with his people: "In all their affliction he was afflicted" (Isa 63:9).

Chapter Israel

Cover

But sharing in affliction is not the only point for why Jesus walks in his people's footsteps. And this is certainly not the point for why this contrast exists between God's displeasure of Israel and pleasure of Jesus. Jesus not only walked in his people's footsteps to identify with their sufferings, he walked in their footsteps as the representative Son of God to *cover* his people. He covers their failures with his victories, their defiant disobedience with his perfect obedience, their sins with his righteousness, and God's displeasure with his fully pleasing merit. He has succeeded where Israel and all of us have failed miserably and repeatedly. Jesus covers every sin and shortcoming with his overwhelming success, triumphs that enable him to save to the uttermost—even from the most grievous of sins. In our worst, Jesus gives his best. And he is able to do all this because he remained sinless even while sharing our sufferings. He waded through the deepest mud, and pulled us out with no mud sticking to him.

Jesus not only can say to us, "I see and share in your sufferings," but he also says, "I can do something about what you are going through."[20] The good news is that the Messiah has come to represent Israel and all the nations before God, to bring us home from the wilderness into which we've all gone astray and where the devil rules, and to take our sins and God's wrath on our behalf. But not only does Jesus block God's wrath, but God will even credit all of Jesus' righteous successes to those who wash their iniquities, disobediences, and failures in the blood of the Lamb of God that takes away the sins of the world!

If that doesn't demonstrate love, I'm not sure what does. What we learn from the parallels of these stories is that Jesus so loved his people that, like Moses (Heb 11:24–25), he willingly chose to suffer with his people and carry every burden of their sins—their grumbling, their testing of God, their defiance, and even their idolatrous worship and grievous breaking of the covenant.

Let all Israel know—the Israel to whom belong the covenants, the promises, the Messiah, the new covenant, and the gospel (Rom 9:4–5)—it was their sins that Jesus suffered and covered, even their worst ones. Jesus does this to the Jew first (Rom 1:16), God's firstborn son.

---

20. Wilder, *Joyful Journey*, 35. This thin but rich book is the most formative resource I've encountered for helping believers grasp how Jesus shares in their suffering and how they can receive the personal healing Immanuel desires to impart.

And let all the nations know that he truly sees us in our very worst; he is with us in our very worst, and he absorbs our worst into himself. Whether Jew or gentile, "all we like sheep *have gone astray*"—wandered our own wildernesses—"we have turned—every one—to his own way; and the Lord has laid on him the iniquity of us all" (Isa 53:6).

What dry and dangerous wilderness, trial, temptation, or test are you facing? Look to Jesus. Abide in Jesus because he already walks with you, beside you. He shares in your wilderness, and he's got it covered.

Chapter David

LIKE MOSES AND LIKE Israel, David also serves as a centerpiece character upon whose story and person Jesus patterned himself. In other words, Jesus imaged David and the events in David's life, and those experiences rippled their way into messianic prophecy. In fact, mirroring David is the starting point for the title "Son of David." It is not merely Jesus' Davidic lineage or the Davidic covenant that this title is concerned with; those are but two drops in a cup that is overflowing with Davidic themes.

When the New Testament refers to Jesus as the "Son of David" (Matt 12:23, 21:9; Luke 18:38), it means for us to understand that Jesus is like David. Just as one can spot the resembling features of a parent in a child, so we are meant to notice Jesus' striking likeness to David. Jesus follows in the footsteps of David, reenacting much of his life story and reflecting his unique person.

So while Davidic lineage tends to get all the attention, it certainly does not exhaust the Son of David connections. David is a person whose story, reputation, anointing, and relationship with God loomed large in the history of Israel. Therefore, "Son of David" is a whole person package deal, not only a matter of physical descent. This chapter explores some of the overlooked but by no means insignificant ways Jesus reflected David. Now, there is so much in David's life and story that makes it into Jesus' own context and experiences, and I certainly cannot cover it all. But for the content we will explore, it will be a deep dive into great detail.

In part one of this chapter, we will consider the parallel contexts just prior to David's and Jesus' coming. Then we will focus on one of the key Bible stories David is most famous for: his bold confrontation with the giant Goliath. We will plunge into a *re*reading of David and Goliath because I think we often miss the real punch line of this story, which I believe is flowing with messianic prophecy. We will explore key flashbacks woven into this beloved story, and in part two, how they develop into one of the most famous prophecies in all the Bible. Finally, in part three, we will veer a bit from David's story to consider how story ripples make their way into the New Testament. Then we will return to 1 Sam 17 to discuss in depth the final and prophetic flashback.

As a head's up, because David's life and story is so central and rich in messianic themes, I found it necessary to focus on both parallelism and ripples to uncover the layers of poetic and often hidden connections to Jesus. Additionally, because the parallels and ripples are countless and complex, I organize this chapter differently by following the biblical storyline itself and simply pointing out where parallels and ripples are present.

PART ONE

The context for a king of Israel actually begins with Moses. He is the one who provided the divine stipulations for the kind of king Israel was to have. The full description is found in Deut 17:14–20, but the passage begins with and revolves around one leading qualification: "When you enter the land the LORD your God is giving you and have taken possession of it and settled in it, and you say, 'Let us set a king over us like all the nations around us,' be sure to appoint over you a king the LORD your God chooses" (17:14–15 NIV).

Because Israel's king was to be different from the kings of the nations around them, he must be one whom "the Lord your God chooses" (Deut 17:15). This key phrase is a theme that will become central to the book of Samuel, which is about the arrival of God's chosen king. This is the supreme instruction Moses says Israel was to look out for—namely, *God* will do the choosing of his king. Just keep that in mind for now.

MESSIANIC BEGINNINGS: PARALLELS BETWEEN SAMUEL AND JOHN THE BAPTIST

The book of 1 Samuel opens with a barren woman (no surprise here), Hannah, who comes to Shiloh and pours out her heart before the Lord about having a son. Pleased with her prayer and sacrifice, the Lord not only gives her a son, but he gives her a very important and priestly son who gets to serve as the last prophetic judge before Israel receives her king. Samuel is set apart for the Lord and grows up to be the one who both *identifies* and *anoints* the king of God's choice (1 Sam 16:12–13).

If this story gives you a sense of déjà vu, then you're picking up on the Bible's story ripples! The Gospel of Luke also opens with the famous account of a barren woman from a priestly line (along with her husband, Zechariah, who has prayed for a child) who gives birth not just to any son but Israel's final prophet whose destiny it will be to *announce* and *anoint* the true King of Israel in the waters of the Jordan (John 1:29–34; Matt 3:13–17).

To get even more specific, 1 Samuel and Luke *both* open with the following parallels:

1. A childless case (1 Sam 1:1–2 and Luke 1:5–7)
2. A prayer in a holy place followed by an encounter with a holy person who speaks good news regarding the request (1 Sam 1:10–17 and Luke 1:8–19)
3. A divine granting of the prayer (1 Sam 1:19–20, 27 and Luke 1:13)
4. A similar praise/song that is messianic in nature (1 Sam 2:1–10 and Luke 1:67–79)
5. The coming of a son devoted to the Lord and forerunner to the king of Israel (1 Sam 1:28; 2:35 and Luke 1:76–80; 3:2–6), who later leads the people in returning to God, confessing sin, and even using water to cleanse (1 Sam 7:2–6 and Matt 3:1–3, 5–6)
6. The privilege of this son to identify and anoint God's king (1 Sam 16:12 and John 1:29)

I have listed the parallel passages so you can read them for yourself, as I will not be going into further detail. But I encourage you to flip between the cross-references because the parallels are so striking. Through these stories, we understand that John the Baptist comes in the picture of Samuel, the forerunner preparing the people for God's king. As Samuel was to David, so John the Baptist was to the Son of David.

RE-READING DAVID AND GOLIATH AS MESSIANIC PROPHECY

Unfortunately, because the story of David and Goliath is so familiar to us, and perhaps because the children's department has claimed it as the ultimate children's Bible story, believers tend to miss the fact that this beloved story is messianic prophecy that Jesus fulfills. It is prophecy in story form!

As much as we love and need to teach this story to children, it is *not* primarily a children's story. So, let us put to the side the children's version and tone of this story—and even the immediate spiritual application to our own lives and our "giants" for now—and instead ready our minds to be on the lookout for patterns and similarities to other stories, persons, and events in the Bible.

Flashbacks and foreshadowing are the building blocks of Bible prophecy. Flashbacks to the past often open prophetic portals that foreshadow or build something in the future. In the story of David and Goliath found in 1 Sam 17, we will stumble upon three important flashbacks to past stories and persons. We will trace these flashbacks and examine how they foreshadow the messianic future.

Because these flashbacks are integrated within the story and its flow, reading the actual story cannot be bypassed. Therefore, please take sufficient time to read through 1 Sam 17, even if you already know the story. Read it this time with an investigative mind looking for clues to possible flashbacks. As I said, there are three major connections to other familiar stories and significant persons in Israel's history before David.

Let's also be reading with this question in mind: What in this story is similar to what I already know about Jesus? After all, we modern readers have the privilege of not just tracing the shadows of the Messiah from the Old Testament but also seeing the fulfillment of those foreshadowings in the gospels. It will be key to remember that David is chosen as God's first royal messiah (anointed one) to build the prophetic profile of God's ultimate Messiah, Jesus the Son of David. Let's first briefly trace some messianic parallels between David and Jesus before diving into the three major flashbacks.

Hidden Saviors and Unlikely Kings

As Bible readers with the advantageous lens to look backward and forward at the same time, one of the first connections to notice about David and Jesus is that they are both hidden saviors and unlikely kings. Judging by externals, David was a shepherd boy. He is not described as tall and kingly like Saul was when elected king (1 Sam 9:2). So when this young shepherd boy enters onto the front lines of battle with Goliath, he doesn't look much like a saving solution to Israel's dire predicament.[1]

It's similar with Jesus. He didn't arrive looking like a messianic king or savior. Not only did Jesus come as God in the humble form of a vulnerable human being, but he *didn't* choose to come as a military leader, a priest in the temple, a Pharisee, Sadducee, or scribe. He was not even a ruler of a synagogue. In fact, like David, Jesus held no status. Just as David was known and associated as Jesse's shepherd boy (1 Sam 16:11, 19; 17:15, 28), Jesus was referred to by the people as the carpenter's son (Matt 13:55). These are both very humble, ordinary positions and not exactly the resume you need to apply for kingship—not in the world's eyes, at least.

David was also an unlikely king because he was the youngest of his brothers (1 Sam 16:11; 17:14)—the last brother with the least status. It probably came as a complete shock when God told Samuel to anoint the youngest of the brothers and not the eldest, Eliab (1 Sam 16:6–7). Jesse, the brothers, and even righteous Samuel were likely floored by God's choice for a king.[2] David's chosenness was so out of the ordinary, unpredictable, and unlikely that David's own father didn't even think it necessary for David to be present with the rest of his brothers when Samuel arrived. He left him to tend the sheep (1 Sam 16:10–11).

In Israelite culture, it was the eldest firstborn son who took center stage according to the Torah. The firstborn is preselected for the birthright inheritance (like Esau), and it is the firstborn who is supposed to be dedicated to God: "Consecrate every firstborn male to me, the firstborn from every womb among the Israelites, both man and beast" (Exod 13:2). Because the Torah places this importance on the firstborn son, it is likely everyone thought Eliab, David's oldest brother, would be selected for kingship. Besides, he looked the part. Upon first glance, Samuel felt sure he was the Lord's anointed (1 Sam 16:6). Just like Saul's outer stature had given him automatic status in the eyes of the people (1 Sam 9:1–2), so Eliab's appearance elicited persuasive favor even in the holy eyes of Samuel.

But through the stories of these hidden heroes, we learn that God looks on the hidden heart. In fact, it is the hidden heart that makes a hero, no matter his or her appearance. And when we examine David's and Jesus' heart, we perceive they are men after God's heart. Indeed, a heart after God's heart ought to mark the character of God's anointed one. Jesus' heart would

---

1. Rydelnik and Blum, *Moody Handbook*, 379.
2. Rydelnik and Blum, *Moody Handbook*, 378.

not only reflect David's "after-God's-own-heart" feature, but this heart imagery would reach its apex in Jesus' complete unity and oneness with the Father's heart and will: "I and the Father are one" (John 10:30); "I am in the Father and the Father is in me" (John 14:11); "My food is to do the will of him who sent me and to accomplish his work" (John 4:34); "For I have not spoken on my own authority, but the Father who sent me has himself given me a commandment—what to say and what to speak" (John 12:49).

One of the grandest and most epic displays of David's "after-God's-own-heart" feature is in the story of David and Goliath. This glorious scene is really where we see David's heart beating in strong, syncopated rhythm to God's heart and will—without missing a beat. As such, this story is drafting for us prophecy of God's future Messiah. Let's dive into the first flashback.

Giant Fear: The First Flashback

While the first flashback doesn't exactly fall on one verse, it is signaled to us by 1 Sam 17:11: "On hearing the Philistine's words, Saul and all Israel lost their courage and were terrified." By the time we reach this verse, our minds are supposed to have revisited another incredibly significant time in Israel's history where Israel's mighty military men were again camped out to confront giant enemies but completely lost their courage.

If we were the original Hebrew readers of 1 Samuel 17, this confrontation with a literal giant and Israel's paralyzing fear would immediately send us back to the books of Numbers and Deuteronomy, where we read about Israel's army camped out on the border of the promised land, consumed with giant fear. What did they see when they spied out the land that made them lose all courage?

Giants! The "sons of Anak," or "the Anakites/Anakim," were the descendants of the Nephilim/Rephaim who were literal giants. And Goliath was one of the few remaining descendants of this bloodline that God instructed Israel in the Torah to wipe out.[3]

In the Numbers account, we see specific reference to these giants, and in the Deuteronomy account we really get a sense of Israel's paralyzing fear.

---

3. Heiser, *Unseen Realm*, 228–29. While there are other interpretations of who the Nephilim were, I find Hesier's treatment most convincing and therefore presuppose his analysis in this book. For an overview of the varying positions, check out the following for good summaries: "Who Are the Nephilim," and Cook, "Who Are the Sons of God."

Chapter David

> Then the men who had gone up with him said, "We are not able to go up against the people, for they are stronger than we are." So they brought to the people of Israel a bad report of the land that they had spied out, saying, "The land, through which we have gone to spy it out, is a land that devours its inhabitants, and all the people that we saw in it are of great height. And there we saw *the Nephilim* (the *sons of Anak, who come from the Nephilim*), and we seemed to ourselves like grasshoppers, and so we seemed to them. (Num 13:31–33)

> Our brothers have made *our hearts melt in fear*. They say, "The people are stronger and taller than we are; the cities are large, with walls up to the sky. We even saw *the Anakites* there." Then I said to you, "*Do not be terrified; do not be afraid of them*. The LORD your God, who is going before you, will fight for you, as he did for you in Egypt, before your very eyes, and in the wilderness. There you saw how the LORD your God carried you, as a father carries his son, all the way you went until you reached this place." In spite of this, you did not trust in the LORD your God . . . (Deut 1:28–32 NIV)

Both the giants and the melting fear are replayed in 1 Sam 17. Israel's terrifying confrontation with the giant Goliath is a flashback to Israel's confrontation with the giants on the border of the promised land. It's a similar story, and Israel's response is again similar—fear and distrust!

What's more, in Numbers, Deuteronomy, and 1 Samuel, the giant fear paralyzes Israel's army so that they fail to fight. Echoing the experience in the Torah, Israel's army again refuses to enter into the fight with Goliath because their fear-melted hearts do not trust that the Lord would fight for them (Deut 1:30, 33). In other words, their hearts were not after the Lord's heart. And that void of faith was instead filled with fear. In the book of Numbers, the lack of trust and faith produced disobedience, which cost Israel another forty years in the wilderness. Here in 1 Sam 17, the text records that the army was at the camp listening to Goliath's blasphemous taunts for forty days: "For forty days the Philistine came forward every morning and evening and took his stand" (1 Sam 17:16).

So in 1 Sam 17, here we are all over again. It's a déjà vu moment. All Israel is overcome with terror from their giant enemy and not trusting God to fight for them, not trusting that the battle belongs to the Lord—except for David. David comes to us as a better and more-developed Joshua and Caleb, who protested Israel's fears and told them to take the land saying, "Do not fear the people of the land, for they are bread for us. Their protection is removed from them, and the Lord is with us" (Num 14:9). Joshua and Caleb knew that the Lord had already delivered their enemies into Israel's hands. God looked pleasurably upon their hearts of faith (which were after God's own desires and will) and rewarded them with the promise that they will inherit the land while the rest of their generation will not (Num 14:30).

In the spirit of Joshua and Caleb, David enters this repeat scenario and says to Goliath's towering face, "This day the Lord will deliver you into my hands" and "I will give the carcasses of the Philistine army to the birds and the wild animals" (1 Sam 17:46). And with these famous, bold words reminiscent of Joshua and Caleb's, David ends the flashback to Num 13—or better yet, he picks up the ripple and develops it in a way that redeems the past. Instead of ending the story in failure and tragedy like back in Num 13, David takes on Goliath and rescues not only himself but all Israel from their giant enemy, their giant fears, and their giant disobedience.

Biblically, fear is the opposite of faith. It is a form of unbelief giving way to disobedience that puts God's name at stake, allowing him to be defied in the eyes of his enemies. That's the real problem with fear. As a man in tune with God's heart, David saw what fear was doing to God's name and reputation. He says, "For who is this uncircumcised Philistine, that he should defy the armies of the living God?" (1 Sam 17:26). And later, David confronts Goliath saying, "I come to you in the name of the Lord of hosts, the God of the armies of Israel, *whom you have defied*" (1 Sam 17:45).

In strong contrast to Num 13, David's obedience and faith in 1 Sam 17 covers Israel's disobedience and cowardice and spares all Israel from their enemy *and* God's displeasure. In a way, David's obedience is credited to and extends to all Israel because they all benefit from this great salvation out of the hands of their historic enemy. In David's day, Israel's greatest and unshakable enemy was the Philistines. They were Israel's enemies from long ago—even before Samson was judge! They are mentioned among the nations holding land God commanded Israel to take:

> This is the land that yet remains: all the regions of the Philistines, and all those of the Geshurites (from the Shihor, which is east of Egypt, northward to the boundary of Ekron, it is counted as Canaanite; there are five rulers of the Philistines, those of Gaza, Ashdod, Ashkelon, Gath, and Ekron), and those of the Avvim. (Josh 13:2–3)

Chapter David

The Philistines were the bane of Israel's existence, not quickly or easily defeated. And while Samuel subdued the Philistines from entering the land of Israel (1 Sam 7:13), it was David who finally defeated them and took control of the territories held by their longstanding enemy (2 Sam 8:1, 1 Chr 18:1). In saving the day in 1 Samuel 17, David is delivering Israel from her worst, indefatigable enemy. But he is also redeeming Israel, covering their fears with his faith and their disobedience with his obedience.

Moreover, David alone saves all Israel by going down into the valley of death himself. There at the "Valley of Elah" between the two camps (1 Sam 17:2), David literally descends into "the valley of the shadow of death" (Ps 23:4)—a very real valley, beneath a very real and giant shadow, and a very real confrontation with death—to save his people. David slays his people's greatest enemy who was undefeatable until the arrival of God's unique messiah. In every biblical sense of the word, David *redeems* his people from bondage to their enemies. And he risks his life doing so. Additionally, David accomplishes this sweeping deliverance as not-yet king, but a mere shepherd and errand-boy for his father. He does it all as an unlikely hero and hidden king.

Can you see what's happening—what's developing? These stories are slowly crafting the profile and the resume of the anointed one (messiah) whom God has chosen to cover all Israel's disobedient sins and redeem her from her worst enemy. David's story and person are paving the prophetic pathways the Son of David will tread.

Here in David's story, the past and the future are coming together through flashbacks and foreshadowing. As David covered Israel's disobedience (past and present) with his victorious heroic rescue, so another David will ripple forth—another hidden hero and unlikely king—who will also be victorious in redeeming Israel's disobedience, sins, and failures—including King David's. Indeed, he will be a far greater David.

David's story in this flashback foreshadows a few things about God's ultimate Messiah:

1. He will confront and defeat both Israel's and all humanity's giant, indefatigable enemies as not-yet king and as God's hidden but anointed savior of the world. Interestingly, we first glimpse a stand off between Jesus and the devil taking place in Jesus' forty-day desert testing and taunting from the devil.[4]

---

4. What do you imagine Jesus was thinking about as he endured every one of those forty days in the wilderness testing? Besides his interactions with the devil and the

2. Messiah will completely cover his people's fears and disobedience with the merit of his own obedience and faithfulness to God. And he will accomplish all of this as a hidden, unlikely hero, and not-yet king.

As we will see with the second flashback, this is the work Jesus accomplished by dying on the cross and resurrecting from the dead, defeating the giant enemies of God's people both without (Satan) and within (sin and death).

A Life-Changing Errand: The Second Flashback

The second flashback in the story of David and Goliath has to do with David and his brothers. In 1 Sam 17:14, David is described as the youngest out of his many brothers. Of course, that's not enough for a flashback; we need more than that.[5] And we get more—a lot more. He is the youngest son who is sent by his father to check on the well-being—or "shalom" in Hebrew—of his brothers in Saul's army camped at the Valley of Elah and to send word back to him: ". . . look into the well-being of your brothers and bring back confirmation from them" (1 Sam 17:18 NASB).

Scripture he quoted, I imagine Jesus' thoughts were deeply occupied with these flashbacks of Israel's stories. Surely these stories were near and dear to his heart. As we saw in chapter Israel, Jesus knew he was walking in the footsteps of his people so as to cover their failures with his victories. For each of those forty days in his own desert experience, I picture Jesus remembering Israel's forty-year wilderness wanderings, the forty days of fear and taunting by Goliath, the forty days and nights of the flood waters, and all the other places in the Bible's history where God's people, the peak of his creation, failed and experienced judgment. I picture a Jesus who had the self-awareness that he was walking where Israel walked, identifying with his beloved's weaknesses. He had Israel's past in mind so that he could win her future. With each day, each trial, each temptation and taunt from the devil, he had a story in mind. He would succeed where she failed. He would have firm faith where she caved in to fear. He would fight where she fled. Out of deep, heartfelt love that goes above and beyond, Jesus would win every temptation for every nation on earth, covering all failures and disobedience with his victorious righteousness and empowering obedience. In this way, Jesus fulfills all righteousness (Matt 3:15) for all people. This is what it means that Jesus overcame for you and me. He not only overcame your sin and death on the cross, but he overcame all your giants, temptations, fears, and failures by his obedient life so as to credit you with his perfect righteousness.

5. It is of utmost importance to note that there needs to be sufficient literary evidence within a text to warrant a connection and to protect against bad allegorical interpretations. On this subject, I again recommend Chase, *40 Questions*, as well as Schnittjer and Harmon, *How to Study*.

CHAPTER DAVID

Who else in Israel's history was the youngest son sent by his father to check on his older brothers' well-being and bring back word—and, I might add, whose life was forever changed through this task? Joseph.

> And Israel said to Joseph, "Are your brothers not pasturing the flock in Shechem? Come, and I will send you to them." And he said to him, "I will go." Then he said to him, "Go now and see about the *welfare* of your brothers and the welfare of the flock, and bring *word* back to me." (Gen 37:13–14, NASB)

These two accounts are parallels because this is the point where Joseph's life takes a drastic and providential turn. With this purposeful flashback to Joseph in David's story, the author is now asking us to read David (and especially what happens next in 1 Sam 17) with Joseph and his story in the back of our minds. David's life, too, will encounter a drastic—and deadly—turn of events by this simple errand. Ironically, even though Joseph and David are both sent to check on the shalom (peace, well-being, harmony) of their brothers, what unfolds is the exact opposite of shalom.

Let's keep going in 1 Sam 17. David hears Goliath's taunts when he first arrives and begins inquiring what will be done for the man who kills this Philistine who dares defy the armies of the living God (1 Sam 17:26). Then we observe David's interaction with his older brother, Eliab. It is not a very pleasant encounter, but we may have already suspected that knowing the story of Joseph and his interaction with his brothers upon arriving in Shechem.

Eliab hears David's question, and immediately his anger burns against David: "'Why did you come down here?' he asked. 'Who did you leave those few sheep with in the wilderness? *I know your arrogance and your evil heart*—you came down to see the battle!' 'What have I done now?' protested David. 'It was just a question'" (1 Sam 17:28–29 HCSB).

This isn't your usual tough love and brotherly teasing. For whatever reason that we're not really given, Eliab's mockery, anger, and cruel accusation reveal that David is seriously despised in the eyes of his quite bitter brother—like Joseph was despised in the eyes of his brothers. Some have connected Eliab's sharp reaction to his own shame of failing to volunteer to fight Goliath while others say it simply reveals a long-standing tension between the brothers.[6] While these may all be true, I believe Eliab's bitterness and the intensity of it centers around the fact that, just one chapter

---

6. Rydelnik and Blum, *Moody Handbook*, 380.

ago, Samuel had anointed David as God's king over and above all the other seemingly more-qualified older brothers, especially Eliab, the firstborn, whom even Samuel thought God had chosen (1 Sam 16:6). And in fact, the text says that Samuel anointed David "in the presence of his brothers" (1 Sam 16:13). This scene is strikingly similar to when Jacob adorned Joseph with a fancy robe, thus favoring him over his brothers (Gen 37:3).[7] And "when his brothers saw that their father loved him more than all his brothers, they hated him and could not speak peacefully to him" (37:4). This episode is then immediately followed by Joseph's prophetic dream of ruling over his brothers (37:5–10), thus setting him apart even more not only as Jacob's favored son but now as God's chosen ruler. Additionally, this royal-like elevating of Joseph takes place right before the life-changing errand (37:12–14)—just like in David's story, whose anointing precedes his own life-altering errand (1 Samuel 16).

In other words, David's storyline in 1 Sam 16–17 is being recorded and recited to us according to Joseph's storyline. Samuel's royal anointing of David (1 Sam 16) and Jacob's adorning of Joseph with the robe (and the dream of rulership) both immediately precede this life-changing errand. And in both plots, a negative exchange with jealous brothers immediately follows the errand. Coincidence? No, it's literature. It's the creative genius behind good literature. We are meant to catch the connections between Joseph and David. They are both despised in the eyes of their brothers who are envious of the youngest son's chosenness.

Notice what Eliab accuses David of: "arrogance" and an "evil heart" (1 Sam 17:28 HCSB). We are supposed to read this as a hard tension because we know God himself has already judged David's heart and declared it to be one "after his own heart," a key quality marking David fit to be king in God's eyes. Eliab's accusation not only couldn't be further from the truth, but it carries a tone of jealousy, hatred, and rejection of David. There is a Joseph-like brotherly envy happening between David and his brother. So we have this sharp contrast and tangible tension in a major flashback: David, the youngest brother, was chosen and anointed by God to rule as king yet is despised and rejected by his brothers, just like Joseph—also the youngest—was despised and rejected by his brothers yet chosen by God to rule over his brothers (as Joseph's prophetic dream predicted in Gen 37:5–8).

---

7. In a brief email correspondence, Hebrew Bible scholar Robert Alter noted the robe (*ketonit passim*) Jacob gives Joseph is identified in the story of the rape of Tamar as raiment for princesses (2 Sam 13:18), so it would correspond to the clandestine anointment of David in 1 Sam 16.

Chapter David

In both of these important Bible stories, God's chosen one is despised and rejected by his own flesh and blood, his own kinsmen. Perhaps now it makes a bit more sense why Jesus insisted to his disciples that he *had* to suffer and be rejected by his brothers, his own people. Luke 9:22 records Jesus emphasizing this very point: "The Son of Man must suffer many things and be rejected by the elders and chief priests and scribes, and be killed, and on the third day be raised." And in John 1:11 it says, "He came to his own, and his own people did not receive him." Knowing that David and Joseph are building the prophetic profile of God's messiah, verses like these in the gospels begin to make more sense. These Old Testament stories serve as a template by which Israel could recognize her messianic king, who will and *must* share in David's experiences. And the fact that David shares in Joseph's experiences prophetically foreshadows that the Messiah and Son of David will also be despised and rejected by his own.

Now, it ought to be mentioned that this despised-and-rejected pattern ripples throughout the entire Scripture (consider just about every prophet). It did not begin with Joseph and it did not stop with David. We also observe it with Moses, another key ruling figure in Israel's history. Although chosen by God, he too was despised and rejected on multiple occasions by the very ones he was sent to deliver—his own people. Moses' leadership was challenged and rejected all throughout the wilderness wanderings (Num 16:1–40). Yet, like David in 1 Samuel 17, Moses interceded to save the lives of his people (Num 14:10–20; Deut 9:13–29). However, I believe this ripple first began in the garden, when God's own image-bearers first despised and rejected God himself and his rule with the first sin. Since then, we observe this contrast of being *chosen by God* but *despised by people* in many of the great biblical leaders, rulers, and prophets God raised up.

But when we observe this theme in David, God's first messiah and king of Israel, we can certainly expect it in the Messiah and King of Kings. Jesus was likewise despised and rejected by his own family and his people but also chosen and exalted by God as king over them.

But not only will Jesus be despised and rejected, he will also be condemned to death by the leadership of his day. That is also something we can expect because it, too, was foreshadowed in both Joseph's and David's stories. On the heels of being despised and rejected, both Joseph and David are condemned to death by Israel's leadership in their day. Whether a pit or a valley, Joseph and David both descend into the shadow of death (which is then followed by a rescue).

Joseph

Joseph's brothers were not just brothers. They represent the twelve tribes of Israel and are therefore the authoritative elders or leadership of God's people, especially after Jacob's passing. Moreover, as soon as they see Joseph in the distance, the brothers actively plot and condemn Joseph to death like a council would gather to discuss and execute a judgement.

Driven by green envy, they say to one another, "Here comes this dreamer. Come now, let us kill him and throw him into one of the pits" (Gen 37:20). Reuben disagrees saying "Let us not take his life. . . . Shed no blood; throw him into this pit here in the wilderness, but do not lay a hand on him" (37:21–22). They agree, and after holding Joseph in a pit like a king would hold a prisoner in a dungeon, Judah then suggests another sentencing: "Come, let us sell him to the Ishmaelites" (37:27). Although he is technically rescued from death, nevertheless, Joseph's life changes forever, and it won't be until much, much later that we see a bigger rescue unfold. Ironically, it will be Joseph doing the rescuing. His sufferings will bring about a great salvation.

By the way, when Joseph comes to his brothers, they first strip him of his robe, the robe of many colors that he wore (Gen 37:23). This "stripping of the robe" imagery can be compared and paralleled with Matt 27:28 where the Roman soldiers "stripped off Jesus' clothes and put a scarlet robe on him." Considering the fact that Joseph's robe signaled his favored status from his brothers—and potentially his authority over them[8]—this stripping becomes strikingly prophetic of Jesus, the ultimate exalted yet rejected brother. Moreover, as Joseph was sold by his brothers for twenty pieces of silver (Gen 37:28), so Jesus got sold out by his own disciple, Judas, for thirty pieces of silver (Matt 26:15).

David

In 1 Sam 17, we see David also being sent to his death by King Saul, Israel's leadership, shortly after his being despised and rejected by his brother, Eliab. But as in the first flashback, David surprises us with a new twist and departure to the familiar pattern in Joseph. An interesting development in David's story is that David freely *volunteers* to fight Goliath (1 Sam 17:32). This doesn't take away the fact that Saul still leads a shepherd boy to his

---

8. See the note on Gen 37:3 in Barry et al., *Faithlife Study Bible*.

Chapter David

death by sending him to do a job Saul himself is responsible for as king. But such courageous willingness on David's part to lay down his life for his people sprouts forth a new ripple in the profile of God's Messiah, one that both foreshadows and finds its fulfillment in Jesus' words: "No one takes [my life] from me, but I lay it down of my own accord" (John 10:18).

Also, keeping in mind that David is a literal shepherd who volunteers to fight Goliath and who even risked his life fighting lions and bears for his literal sheep (1 Sam 17:34–37), it makes more sense that Jesus would say, "I am the good shepherd. The good shepherd lays down His life for the sheep" (John 10:11).

But the thing to notice here is that Saul, who represents the head leadership in Israel at this time, sends David off to his death rather than fighting Goliath himself. Again, this was the king's responsibility, as he is the commander in chief. From Saul's point of view, it's not at all likely that he believes David will actually succeed.[9] Saul hasn't displayed any faith, confidence, or courage this entire forty days of Philistine defiance. Moreover, by this point, Saul's perpetual disobedience had already cost him the kingdom (1 Sam 15:28). So when Saul tells David "Go, and may the LORD be with you" (1 Sam 17:37 NASB), it is not a prayer of hope but parting words of a final farewell. Saul likely has zero confidence he will ever see David again.[10] But instead of countering David and letting the shame of this shepherd boy's courage jolt him into a sense of kingly duty, Saul allows it all to unfold.

So, in sending David to fight in the Valley of Elah between the two camps (1 Sam 17:2), the head leadership of Israel was quite literally sending God's chosen and anointed one into "the valley of the shadow of death" (Ps 23:4)—which, again, was a very real valley, beneath a very real and giant shadow, and a very real confrontation with death. Later on, after David's victory and raging popularity, a disturbingly envious Saul will devote the rest of his life in hot pursuit of David's life. As with Joseph's brothers, envy drives Saul to madly seek the life of God's chosen messiah.

Jesus

As you have already connected, these story ripples expand and escalate to foreshadow the rejection and condemnation of God's ultimate Messiah and the Son of David by the Sanhedrin, the head Jewish leadership in Jesus'

---

9. Rydelnik and Blum, *Moody Handbook*, 381.
10. Rydelnik and Blum, *Moody Handbook*, 381.

day: "Then the chief priests and the elders of the people gathered in the palace of the high priest, whose name was Caiaphas, and plotted together in order to arrest Jesus by stealth and kill him" (Matt 26:3–4). Moreover, what drove these leaders to plot their fellow brother's death was the same all-consuming envy already witnessed: "For [Pilate] knew that it was out of envy that they had delivered [Jesus] up" (Matt 27:18).

Because this despised-and-rejected pattern is so prevalent in the lives and stories of so many of God's anointed people (including Israel as a nation, who often found herself despised and rejected by the surrounding nations and empires), this pattern ripples into a full-blown prophecy of the Messiah in the days of the prophets, taking center stage in Isaiah.

PART TWO

ISAIAH'S SUFFERING SERVANT: A JOSEPH-LIKE DAVID

Isaiah 53 is that fully-developed prophetic ripple of an ultimate Joseph-like David, who is chosen and anointed by God to rule as king but who will be despised, rejected, and condemned to death. And yet, he will:

- victoriously conquer that rejection and death in the name of the LORD like David;
- lavishly pardon unthinkable betrayal like Joseph;
- save many lives through suffering like both Joseph and David;
- and rule as king in Israel like David as well as a Savior over the nations like Joseph back in Egypt.

All of these features get woven into this great, poetic chapter. In a way, it's the poetry and the power of story that makes Isa 53 prophetic. It's genius—pure, creative genius.

It is absolutely key to see that this famous prophecy is not a stand-alone prediction about the future that is isolated from Israel's past (which is how many tend to read it and even ask others to read it); rather, this prophecy stands on the firm foundation of story—prophetic histories within the Bible that Jesus enters into and fulfills as Israel's Messiah.[11]

---

11. It is worth noting there exist other ripples and themes besides the ones discussed that also have developed and get imported into this prophecy—especially patterns and images featured in the Passover story and the tabernacle/temple. One example is the atoning sacrifice of a lamb that Isaiah weaves into Isa 53:7. Clearly, the lamb image is

Chapter David

The basic template of Isa 53 is about the familiar biblical experience of enduring gross rejection and unjust condemnation, even unto death, and yet miraculously coming out on the other side as a victorious overcomer and savior of many people. And when we follow the structural flow (or storyline) of Isa 53, we hear echoes of the same themes and patterns we've been examining in Joseph and David.

In summary, this great chapter begins with a description of 1) an unlikely, hidden hero chosen by God himself. Then it bleeds into 2) the sufferings of that chosen servant. Finally, the prophecy ends with 3) the spoils of the suffering-yet-sucessful victor.

1) An Unlikely, Hidden Hero: Isaiah 53:1-2, NASB

> Who has believed our report?
> And to whom has the arm of the LORD been revealed?
> For He grew up before Him like a tender shoot [some translations say "like a young plant"]
> And like a root out of dry ground;
> He has no stately form or majesty
> That we would look at Him,
> Nor an appearance that we would take pleasure in Him.

"A tender shoot" or "young plant" coming out of "dry ground" is greatly reminiscent of Joseph and David who were both youth and the youngest of their brothers and therefore, in that culture, the least of them. This language also harkens back to Isaiah's messianic prophecy in 11:1 of a coming "shoot from the stump of Jesse [David's father], a branch from his roots" that will "bear fruit."

Additionally, the "ground" often serves as symbolic agricultural imagery for the womb. We know Joseph was born to Rachel, who was Jacob's favorite wife but whose womb was *dry* (barren) for the longest time until God opened it. So Joseph's birth was like a plant supernaturally taking root in dry, infertile ground. As we've seen, this kind of birth (out of barrenness)

---

a central biblical ripple that finds fulfillment in John's introduction of Jesus: "Behold the lamb of God that takes away the sins of the world" (John 1:29). While my focus in this section is limited to the messianic ripples of Joseph's and David's life stories, it is important to acknowledge that these other existing ripples have their own stories to tell and deserve their own study.

is immensely familiar and prevalent throughout Israel's history, beginning with the first matriarch, Sarah herself.

From the beginning, conceiving out of barrenness was meant to signal the supernatural hand of God putting important events and promises into motion, as I explained in chapter Abraham: "Barren to Bearing." This theme is a forerunner heralding the message, "Look out! God is on the move!" And we see it rippling into Joseph's story and Isa 53, where it compounds with David and finds fulfillment in Jesus, the righteous branch from the stump of Jesse, who was born taking root not just in a dry, barren womb, but in a dry, *virgin* womb. Conceiving in a virgin womb is even more impossible than a barren one. God definitely upped the sign and miracle there.

"He has no *stately* form or *majesty* that we would *look* at Him, nor an *appearance* that we would take *pleasure* in Him" (53:2). All of this is royal language sending us straight into the book of 1 Samuel where we read all about God's shocking choice for a king and messiah, David. Words like "stately form," "majesty," and "appearance" that is pleasing remind us of King Saul who possessed impressive physical stature (1 Sam 9:2, 10:23) yet was rejected by God because of his inner waywardness (1 Sam 13:13–14, 15:11). It also reminds us of Eliab, the eldest of Jesse's sons whom Samuel merely *looked* upon and assumed he was God's anointed because of his pleasing appearance.

As we learned, David is a strong contrast. God's chosen servant (Isa 52:13) might not appear to look like a king or savior, but he certainly possesses the right heart, which is what makes the hero and gets God's attention (1 Sam 16:7). This Davidic picture of humility develops its way into Isaiah's portrait of the suffering servant.

2) The Sufferings of the Servant: Isaiah 53:3–9

The next section, verses 3–9, transitions into the sufferings of this servant of the LORD. Below, I've included only a selection of these verses.

> He was despised and rejected by men,
> A man of sorrows and acquainted with grief...
> He was oppressed, and he was afflicted...
> By oppression and judgment he was taken away...
> cut off out of the land of the living...
> And they made his grave with the wicked...
> although he had done no violence,

Chapter David

and there was no deceit in his mouth.

We already learned how both Joseph and David are despised and rejected and even judged and condemned by men. But to be more specific, these words and imagery recall a despised and rejected Joseph literally being *taken away* in bondage by slaveholders and *cut off* from the promised land of his father and family, where he not only grew up but where he experienced life and freedom. What shattering *sorrow* and grisly *grief* Joseph knew.

But the *oppression* wouldn't stop there. In Egypt, he would also be falsely accused of raping Potiphar's wife (Gen 39:14-15) and put in prison as "with the wicked" (53:9), "although he had done no violence, and there was no deceit in his mouth" (53:9). Joseph not only suffered injustice as an innocent victim, but he suffered because of his righteousness—because he held to his integrity and God's will. And while he is not the only one, the Bible seems to spotlight Joseph for this kind of suffering, especially considering the lengthy pages and attentive detail the book of Genesis devotes to Joseph's woes.

This section is also supposed to trigger in our minds David being cut off from the very land over which he is supposed to reign as king because of Saul's oppressive and unrelenting pursuit of him, forcing David to go into hiding even in enemy territory—Gath, the very land and home of Goliath (1 Sam 27:1-4, 1 Sam 17:4)! Even after David becomes king, he is later forced to flee from his own land and from his own son, Absalom, who conspires against David and even wins the hearts of the people of Israel (2 Sam 15:13-14).

Before we move on, we should first ask, what purpose does this Servant's suffering serve? How does the ancient Hebrew mind make sense of evil, pain, and suffering that God providentially allows in the lives of his loved and chosen people?

In Gen 37, Joseph provides us with the proper biblical worldview: "What you intended against me for evil, God intended for good, in order to accomplish a day like this—to preserve the lives of many people" (Gen 50:20). Earlier in Gen 45, Joseph also makes sense of all he suffered by saying God used his brothers' betrayal to send him (Joseph) ahead of them "to save lives" (45:5) "by a great deliverance" (45:7). Similarly, this ultimate Suffering Servant is crushed and put to grief by the providential hand of the LORD (53:10) and stricken for his people (53:8) in order to "make many to be accounted righteous" (53:11), to preserve and save lives (*eternally!*) by a great or, rather, *greater* deliverance.

3) The Servant's Spoils: Isaiah 53:10–12, NASB

Isaiah 53 ends with the spoils/victory Joseph and David are both known for:

> ... the good pleasure of the LORD will prosper in His hand.
> As a result of the anguish of His soul,
> He will see *it and* be satisfied;
> By His knowledge the Righteous One,
> My Servant, will justify the many,
> For He will bear their wrongdoings.
> Therefore, I will allot Him a portion with the great,
> And He will divide the plunder with the strong,
> Because He poured out His life unto death,
> And was counted with wrongdoers.

Consider "the good pleasure of the LORD will prosper in His hand" (53:10). In this important, hope-packed theological claim, we again hear the earliest echoes of Joseph's rich and redeeming words: "What you intended for evil, God meant for good." God's will shall prosper out of deep suffering. But even more so, we can almost feel God's power prospering in David's literal hand as he throws the stone and takes down Goliath with "the arm of the LORD" (Isa 53:1). I believe such echoes are not only present but intentional. We're supposed to hear them, *feel* them.

Now look at "As a result of the anguish of His soul, He will see *it and* be satisfied" (53:11). Here we can almost feel both the anguish and satisfaction in Joseph's words at the naming of his second son, Ephraim: "God has made me fruitful in the land of my affliction" (Gen 41:52). What a hopeful statement. What good news. God knows how to reward intense affliction. He knows how to satisfy the deepest anguish with an eternal weight of glory that far outweighs every second of our suffering. He knows how to redeem the dark night of the soul.

We can also almost hear David's sigh of satisfaction in seeing the proud Goliath fall. At long last, justice is served. Wicked enemies are humbled and outwitted. Defiant taunts are silenced. Once again, God turned curses and evil intentions into a blessing that saved many lives.

Chapter David

Now let's look at "By His knowledge the Righteous One, My Servant, will justify the many, For He will bear their wrongdoings" (Isa 53:11). Joseph suffers the sins of his brothers for many grueling years. And then he forgives his brothers. In pardoning them, Joseph is acquitting them of guilt, not holding it against them. Joseph's remarkable absolution of his brothers is one of the earliest biblical pictures for God's justifying forgiveness. Besides forgiving them, Joseph also gives them a new life in Egypt, abundant in provision to save them from the literal famine ravaging the land (Gen 45:10–11). In forgiving us, Jesus not only justifies us but also gives us a new and abundant life (John 10:10), promising to provide for our every need (Matt 6:26, 31–33).

Similarly, David redeems Israel by interceding for her and facing the enemy as her righteous representative and God's servant, covering Israel from her failures and fears—past and present. David defeats Goliath and death while the people stand by helplessly in their worst fears and disobedient failures toward God (by failing to fight). So, too, *while* we were yet God's enemies, living in fear and disobedience, Messiah willingly descended into the valley of death for us and conquered Satan, hell, and death itself (Rom 5:8).

Finally, think about "Therefore I will allot Him a portion with the great . . ." (Isa 53:12). This is the story of David's life. God pulled David out of herding sheep and made him a prince over his people, giving him a throne, a house, and a kingdom that will last forever. God reminds David of exactly these points in the famous chapter on the Davidic covenant: "I took you from the pasture, from tending the flock, and appointed you ruler over my people Israel. I have been with you wherever you have gone, and I have cut off all your enemies from before you. Now I will make your name *great*, like the names of the greatest men on earth" (2 Sam 7:8–9 NIV). David's portion and name would not only be allotted earthly greatness but also heavenly greatness: "Your house and your kingdom will endure *forever* before me; your throne will be established *forever*" (2 Sam 7:16 NIV). God's promise to David that the Messiah would come from his "house" (lineage) and hold the title "the Son of David" is an inheritance of eternal greatness in heaven and on earth. This Davidic greatness is escalated and fulfilled in Jesus' allotted portion: ruling authority in heaven and on earth (Matt 28:18).

In conclusion, the structure of Isa 53 plays off of past stories and the lives of other important servants of the Lord to foreshadow a future servant who shares in and fulfills the biblical experience of immense suffering and redeeming victory. While David and Joseph are central, especially as David is God's first chosen messiah, the story ripples behind Isa 53 go beyond Joseph and David. All of God's anointed prophets share in the spirit of Isa 53 to various degrees when they, too, put their lives on the line for the sake of a people who despised and rejected them and their message.

When we read Isa 53, I don't believe we're supposed to first think ahead about one future person. Our minds ought to flood with flashbacks to the ones who were used by God to build and develop this prophecy—other suffering servants caught up in the ripple effect. Our minds and memories are to draw on their stories of sufferings, their rejections, their exiles, and their deliverances—which the Suffering Servant comes to share in and take upon himself in a way that is far, far greater than any of those previously anointed servants. In sharing in their stories of sorrow, he identifies with his people. This is what the writer of Hebrews was getting at: "For we do not have a high priest who is unable to sympathize with our weaknesses, but one who in every respect has been tempted as we are, yet without sin" (Heb 4:15).

This Messiah comes in their picture. His story grows out of a previous, familiar ripple. But he also introduces a new twist and development to the story: he comes without sin. He shares in these stories but without sin, and that single-handedly makes him the greater Joseph, the greater David, and the better Moses. He is the Servant of servants, the King of kings, the Prophet of prophets, and like Israel, the greater firstborn Son. That sinlessness sets him apart from his people in terms of character and the Law but not in terms of story and experiences. As we learned in chapter Israel, it makes him worthy and able to cover his people's transgressions, bear their sorrows, and make the proper guilt offering for making many righteous (Isa 53:10–11)—people from the past and in the future. So even as he identifies with his people in their sorrows, he is at the same time atoning for their sins.

PART THREE

For the most part, this book has focused on how stories in the Hebrew Scripture build and develop messianic prophecy. But did you know that New Testament theology and spirituality are also rooted in story ripples?

Sharing in Jesus' story and experiences is a major assumption of the New Testament authors. But sharing in Jesus' story also means partaking in

Israel's experiences, the great men and women of old in the Bible, because Jesus shared in their stories.

It might seem like an out-of-place disruption, but I intentionally want to pause our study of flashbacks in 1 Sam 17 here because one of the central ripples all followers of Jesus enter into is this prophetic "suffering servant" portrait we just explored in the lives of Joseph, David, and Jesus. Although the latter fulfills the prophecy, it remains a ripple effect into which all of God's children are pulled into—God's people from the past, present, and future.

NEW TESTAMENT THEOLOGY

The suffering servant ripple is how New Testament writers, including the apostle Paul, explain so much New Testament theology and spiritual living. Peter explicitly says in his epistle not to be surprised when the "fiery trial" comes upon us but to "rejoice inasmuch as you *participate in the sufferings of Christ*, so that you may be overjoyed when his glory is revealed" (1 Pet 4:12–13). And Paul says the same thing: "The sufferings of Christ overflow to *us*" (2 Cor 1:5). Lest you think this is merely a few verses or a matter of poetic language, here are some other New Testament texts:

- "Blessed are you when others revile you and persecute you and utter all kinds of evil against you falsely on my account. Rejoice and be glad, for your reward is great in heaven, for *so they persecuted the prophets who were before you*" (Matt 5:11–12).
- "We always carry around in our body *the death of Jesus*, so that the *life of Jesus may also be revealed in our body*" (2 Cor 4:10 NIV).
- "Do you not know that *all of us who have been baptized into Christ Jesus were baptized into his death*? We were buried therefore with him by baptism into death, in order that, just as Christ was raised from the dead by the glory of the Father, we too might walk in newness of life. For if *we have been united with him in a death like his, we shall certainly be united with him in a resurrection like his*" (Rom 6:3–5).
- "I want to know Christ—yes, to know the *power of his resurrection and participation in his sufferings, becoming like him in his death, and so, somehow, attaining to the resurrection from the dead*" (Phil 3:10–11 NIV).

- "Since you have been *raised to new life with Christ*, set your sights on the realities of heaven, where Christ sits in the place of honor at God's right hand. For you died to this life, and *your real life is hidden with Christ in God*. And when Christ, who is your life, is revealed to the whole world, you will *share in all his glory*" (Col 3:1, 3–4 NLT).

It's all about sharing stories, sharing experiences—the good and the bad, the triumphs and the struggles. Not only is this at the heart of prophecy, but it is the profound mystery behind the believer's union to the Messiah. Pulled into the current of this never-ending ripple, believers participate in the divine call and anointing to become suffering servants for the sake of others' gain. This is a familiar experience and testimony shared by believers everywhere. It is so ingrained in the believer's thinking; moreover, it's rarely a mindset that needs to be taught. Jesus simply pulls us into his story.

In the text below, notice how Peter draws on Messiah's unjust sufferings to encourage the believers in his day to endure their own unjust suffering:

> Servants, be subject to your masters with all respect, not only to the good and gentle but also to the unjust. For this is a gracious thing, when, mindful of God, *one endures sorrows while suffering unjustly*. For what credit is it if, when you sin and are beaten for it, you endure? But if when you do good and suffer for it you endure, this is a gracious thing in the sight of God. *For to this you have been called, because Christ also suffered for you, leaving you an example, so that you might follow in his steps*. He committed no sin, neither was deceit found in his mouth [a quote from Isa 53:9]. When he was reviled, he did not revile in return; when he suffered, he did not threaten, but continued entrusting himself to him who judges justly. (1 Pet 2:18–23)

Peter uses messianic prophecies from Isa 53 that have already been fulfilled in Jesus to define the believer's call now that they are united to the Messiah. And their call is to be a suffering servant like Jesus was, thereby perpetuating the ancient prophetic ripple. While a controversial verse, Paul also recognizes the believer's basic call to suffer *for others* when he writes, "Now I rejoice in *my sufferings for your sake*, and in my flesh I am filling up what is lacking in Christ's afflictions *for the sake of his body*, that is, *the church*" (Col 1:24). Like Joseph, David, Jesus, Peter, and Paul, we believers are called to walk in the ancient path of suffering as God's servant for the benefit of others. While our sufferings can never make anyone righteous in

Chapter David

the way Jesus' suffering does (Isa 53:11), we can still labor over someone's salvation, like Paul, whose efforts and persecutions benefitted both Jews and gentiles with the gospel.

As believers enter into this union with Messiah and become partakers of the great story and stories of the Bible, we get pulled into the ripple effect of Old Testament imagery, themes, and patterns. In the New Testament, our bodies are called the "temple of the Holy Spirit," the place where God dwells (1 Cor 6:19). We are identified as "priests" who serve, sacrifice, and intercede for the salvation and sake of others (1 Pet 2:9). Jesus calls his disciples the "light of the world" (Matt 5:14), just like he and Israel were and still are. And like Jesus and Israel, we should expect to be despised and rejected by the world—persecuted and perhaps even condemned to death by powerful leaders. Indeed, many believers and martyrs have already followed Jesus on this road to Golgotha. Overall, believers should expect to be treated as Messiah himself was treated, as no servant is greater than his master (John 15:20). This is the inescapable reality of being united to Messiah who was himself united to all Israel and all her anointed servants of the Lord.

Jesus not only takes over our stories when entering into our lives, but we take on *his* story. And through that union, we are grafted into all the stories of the Bible. Whether Jew or gentile, we join in this grand, prophetic story together as one, as our principal identity becomes "in him" (Eph 1:7–14; Gal 3:28).

This oneness in the New Testament is not just between believers alive today or at the same time in history, but in a deep way, we are united as brothers and sisters to Joseph, David, Moses, Joshua, Hannah, Samuel, Esther, Jeremiah, Isaiah, Ezekiel, the disciples, Paul—everyone in the great cloud of witnesses (Heb 12:1). Who are some of your favorite people of faith from the past? Start thinking of them as family. In the kingdom that is coming, they already are.

But for the present, these forerunners of the faith serve as helpful mentors, fathers, and mothers we can look to. We can derive all sorts of encouragement, advice, comfort, and perspective from Joseph's sufferings, David's victories, Abraham's faith, Sarah's laughter, Jacob's wrestling, Moses' leadership, Hannah's prayer, Esther's boldness, Elijah's fears and loneliness, Jonah's disobedience and depression, Israel's wilderness wanderings and many exiles, Jesus' humility, and Paul's chains. They are *all* our brothers and sisters in the Lord. They are a picture of us, and their lives and experiences become a pattern for us, one into which we share.

What is at the very heart of the greatest commandment and golden rule? Is it not *shared experience*? Love *others* as you love *yourself* (Matt 22:39). "Whatever you wish that others would do to you, do also to them, for this is the Law and the Prophets" (Matt 7:12). By the way, this is the very same Law and Prophets Jesus referenced on the road to Emmaus (Luke 24:27). Shared experience is at the heart of how Jesus fulfills the Scriptures. It's all about putting yourself in someone's shoes—their story, their experience—as if it were your own, *making* it your own. It is about bearing someone else's burdens (Gal 6:2), weeping when they weep, rejoicing when they rejoice (Rom 12:15). It's remembering those who are in prison, as though you are in prison with them, and remembering those who are mistreated as though you were feeling their pain, "since you also are in the body" (Heb 13:3). It's all about shared experience in the body of Messiah.

This book is not only about understanding biblical prophecy in the world of the Bible but also perceiving it in your own world, in your own story. If you are united to the Messiah of Israel, then, friend, the prophetic ripples are alive and active in your life, too. As an example, let us consider the prophetic spirit in which Paul wrote 1 Cor 1:26–29, a text plenty of believers identify with and appropriate as their own story:

> Not many of you were wise by human standards; not many were influential; not many were of noble birth. But God chose the foolish things of the world to shame the wise; God chose the weak things of the world to shame the strong. God chose the lowly things of this world and the despised things—and the things that are not—to nullify the things that are, so that no one may boast before him.

Is that your story, your testimony? Well, guess what? Before it was yours, before it was for the Corinthians, it was Israel's story. Do you remember what God told Israel when he first chose her? "The LORD did not set his affection on you and choose you because you were more numerous than other peoples, for you were the *fewest* of all peoples" (Deut 7:7 NIV). And not only the fewest, but the Scriptures go on to talk about how Israel was a stubborn and rebellious people from the start (Exod 32:9, Deut 9:6–7, Jer 7:24–26); not exactly the best qualifications for chosenness (according to human standards). Moreover, the Scriptures describe the other nations around Israel as being mightier and stronger than Israel (Deut 4:38, 9:1–2, Ps 105:12–13).

Chapter David

But there is no text like Ezek 16 for grasping perhaps the most vivid and graphic analogy of Israel's weakness, lowliness, and poverty when God first chose her:

> On the day you were born your cord was not cut, nor were you washed with water to make you clean, nor were you rubbed with salt or wrapped in cloths. No one looked on you with pity or had compassion enough to do any of these things for you. Rather, you were thrown out into the open field, for on the day you were born you were despised. "'Then I passed by and saw you kicking about in your blood, and as you lay there in your blood I said to you, "Live!" I made you grow like a plant of the field. You grew and developed and entered puberty. Your breasts had formed and your hair had grown, yet you were stark naked. "'Later I passed by, and when I looked at you and saw that you were old enough for love, I spread the corner of my garment over you and covered your naked body. I gave you my solemn oath and entered into a covenant with you, declares the Sovereign LORD, and you became mine. (4–8 NIV)

In the gospels, we see this same Spirit—who first chose Israel when she was a naked nobody—continue to choose frail nobodies. In the same spirit of Deuteronomy and Ezekiel, Jesus chooses to set his love, election, and glory on the sick, the sinners, the uneducated, the weakest, and the vulnerable.

Today, in the twenty-first century, God is still choosing the foolish, the weak, the lowly, and the despised things of this world. And the truth is, apart from Jesus, we all match the above descriptions. Even if we are wealthy, educated, and born into nobility, we are naked and empty apart from Jesus. Nothing qualifies us to be chosen or clothed in his salvation.

Abraham, Moses, David, the twelve disciples—all these mighty people were called, chosen, and brought into God's story precisely when they were simple, ordinary folk. Some were even enemies of God. Abraham was an idolater and Moses a murdering fugitive. David was just a shepherd boy, while the disciples were common men and sinners: fishermen, zealots, tax collectors. And the female followers of Jesus were prostitutes (Matt 21:31), fornicators (John 4:18), and demonically oppressed (Luke 8:1–3).

Hopefully you can see the continuity of chosenness from the Old Testament to the New Testament and how the same spirit of the text extends to today, to our own stories. God still moves, acts, and chooses in this same ancient way. So let's conclude with some questions for personal meditation:

1. What themes, patterns, and experiences within Israel's and Jesus' stories have you come to share? Or which people from the Bible do you identify with?
2. How is the spirit of the biblical text prophetically extending into your story and shaping your calling?

THREE ANCIENT PROMISES

The Third Flashback

It's been a while getting here, but at last we've arrived at the third flashback in 1 Sam 17, the story of David and Goliath. I have saved this flashback for the end because it is complex. Really, there are a few prophetic flashbacks that all get compacted into a few sentences. Moreover, these trace all the way back to the garden of Eden. David utters some of the most prophetic words when he famously declares to Goliath,

> You come against me with a dagger, spear, and sword, but I come against you in the name of Yahweh of Hosts, the God of Israel's armies—you have defied Him. Today, the LORD will hand you over to me. Today, I'll strike you down, *cut your head off,* and give the corpses of the Philistine camp to the birds of the sky and creatures of the earth. Then *all the world will know that Israel has a God,* and *this whole assembly will know that it is not by sword or by spear that the LORD saves,* for the battle is the LORD's. He will hand you over to us. (1 Sam 17:45–47 HCSB)

The italicized portions are where the prophetic words or imagery are to be found. I'm going to save the head-cutting imagery for last and first explore the phrases "all the world will know that Israel has a God" and secondly, "all this assembly will know that it is not by sword or spear that the LORD saves." In each of these bold promises, David identifies two different groups of people who will experience two different "knowings." He first addresses all the world (or nations) who will come to know that Israel has a God, or rather, *the* one and only true God.

Chapter David

A Message to the Nations

In the context of 1 Sam 17, David is fighting "as God's servant . . . to reveal [God] to the nations."[12] This of course has long been a task all Israel was entrusted with, and we also observe other key individuals revealing the God of Israel to the nations, like Moses in Egypt (Exod 7:5) and Joshua in conquest of the land (Josh 4:23–24). In chapter Abraham, we studied the first prophetic ripple of God's promise to use Abraham's seed to "bless all the nations of the earth" (Gen 12:3)—and, in fact, to draw the nations back to himself after scattering, disinheriting, and giving them up to other gods. Later, with Moses, we see that ripple expanding as Israel is commissioned to be a light to the nations as a holy nation.

In 1 Sam 17, we are seeing this ancient prophetic promise now getting attached to David, Israel's king. With David, these past prophetic ripples are now being integrated into the profile of the messiah, God's anointed one. By doing this, the biblical author is intentionally foreshadowing that, when God's ultimate anointed king comes, he will be responsible to fulfill this prophetic ripple to its *fullest*. He will distribute the knowledge of the one, true God of Israel to all the nations and begin grafting them back into the inheritance. And, of course, this ripple becomes further developed in the time of the prophets, as we shall shortly see.

When Jesus, the Son of David, commissions his disciples to go into all the nations preaching the good news, he is telling them to spread the (saving) knowledge of the God of Israel. In this commission, he is fulfilling not only David's prophetic words in 1 Sam 17 but every other development of this prophecy that got its start in God's promise to Abraham in Gen 12:3—that all the nations of the earth will be blessed in him.

When Jesus arrives, he inaugurates the new covenant of Jer 31, which, summed up, is all about knowing God: "They shall all know me, from the least of them to the greatest, declares the Lord" (Jer 31:34). Essentially, the way to know if the kingdom of God has come and if the Son of David has arrived is by this key, prophetic sign: when the knowledge of the God of Israel gets distributed to the nations. The fulfillment of this prophecy is no small or easy feat, and historically, it wasn't until Jesus arrived in the first century that such knowledge broke through on an unprecedented global scale via the Great Commission (Matt 28:19–20). With all the enlightenment the nation of Israel has given to the world, they never radiated such a

---

12. Rydelnik and Blum, *Moody Handbook*, 382.

light unto the nations than when the gospel swept over the face of the earth, providing saving knowledge of the God of Israel to every tongue, tribe, people, and nation, generation after generation. And this two-thousand-year-old mission is still ongoing today.

But while the fulfillment of this prophecy got started in Jesus and has accomplished much, the work isn't finished. The prophet Habakkuk lets us know when we can expect the kingdom of God to arrive in its fullness: when "the earth will be filled with the *knowledge* of the glory of the LORD as the waters cover the sea" (Hab 2:14). This verse is one of those more developed prophetic ripples that will find complete fulfillment in the messianic kingdom with Jesus' second coming.

What's interesting to me is that Ps 22—a psalm that is often titled "the Psalm of the Cross" and that begins with the famous words penned by David but cried out by Jesus from the cross, "My God, my God, why have you forsaken me?" (22:1)—this messianic psalm of deep suffering concludes with the prophetic promise that "All the ends of the earth shall remember and turn to the LORD, and all the families of the nations [a direct flashback to Gen 12:3] shall worship before you. For kingship belongs to the LORD, and he rules over the nations" (22:27–28).

What this means is that a major suffering like the one described in Ps 22 will precede the major distribution of the knowledge of God to the nations. While it applies first to king David—it being his psalm about his experiences—we know Jesus entered into David's prophetic suffering described in this psalm and fulfilled its outcome on a greater and fuller messianic level. He first suffered on the cross as God's servant, and then distributed the knowledge of God to the ends of the earth through the Great Commission.

A Message to Israel

Next, let's talk about the other group David prophetically addresses in 1 Sam 17 and the "knowing" they experience:

> all this assembly will know that it is not by sword or spear that the LORD saves. (17:47 HCSB)

Who is "all this assembly" David is talking about? It is all Israel. Specifically and contextually, it is the armies of Israel and its leadership. First Samuel 17:2 goes out of its way to identify Saul and the army: "Saul and the Israelites assembled" at the camp (NIV). Israel and her leadership have been camped out at this battlefront for forty days, cowering in fear and despair at Goliath's taunts.

What is the message Israel and her leaders need to know, according to God's anointed messiah? "It is not by sword or spear that the LORD saves" (1 Sam 17:47 NIV). While this might be a good preaching point for us modern readers, to the original audience, this was a historic and very literal reminder—and partly a rebuke. Unlike the strong, militaristic nations and empires ever surrounding and invading God's people with the most advanced weaponry, this message is not new knowledge for Israel. On the contrary, Israel's entire history and existence has been built upon this message. Yet, it was a message she was constantly learning. And it is a message God continually sent her, even up to the days of Zechariah: "Not by might nor by power, but by my Spirit,' says the LORD Almighty" (Zech 4:6).

In truth, Israel ought to have internalized this message by 1 Sam 17. Think of Moses—he didn't deliver Israel by sword, spear, or any weapon back in Egypt. His weapon was the same as David's weapon here: the name of the LORD (1 Sam 17:45). And even when Israel did fight as warriors under Joshua, God made sure they knew their success was not a result of their human strength or force but because of him—because he had given their enemy into their hand (Josh 2:24; 1 Sam 17:46). There were even times in Israel's history when God intentionally reduced Israel's army, as in the case with Gideon (Judg 7:1–8), so as to drill this message into their minds.

Neither Israel's success nor her salvation ever came by way of the sword, spear, chariots, horses, or human might. Even when other larger empires conquered Israel seemingly through their military capacity, it was only because God had allowed it and even warned of their coming if Israel remained unrepentant (2 Kgs 17:1–21; Isa 9:7–20; Jer 2:33–37). In those tragic cases, God removed his protection from his own people rather than their enemies. So, what David utters here in 1 Sam 17 is one out of *many* lessons. But each of these lessons in Israel's past becomes part of a prophetic ripple effect that keeps developing and extending.

And what David is doing in 1 Sam 17 is actually prophesying that God will bring a wondrous salvation to Israel not through a warrior but a hidden and unlikely hero—like a shepherd boy. So if this is how God's first messiah and king arrives on the scene to defeat Israel's worst enemy, then we ought to get the hint that this familiar pattern is how God's ultimate Messiah and King of Kings will also arrive on the scene in the future. He will not come as a military soldier defeating Israel's greatest and cosmic enemy through sword or spear. Rather, he will come as David, in the name of the LORD. "Blessed is he who comes in the name of the LORD" (Ps 118:26)!

In 1 Sam 17, no one was able to detect God's chosen messiah through mere appearances. But he could be discerned through the hidden heart, which would shine through his works. Similarly, God's future Messiah would not be recognized through appearances or status but discerned by the name and strength of the LORD upon his heart and works.

Using the story of David, later biblical authors and prophets build the messianic profile of a shepherd-king (see Ezek 34:23) who would one day bring an incredible salvation to Israel in an equally astounding, mouth-dropping way: not through the expected might of the military or men, but clothed in the full, miracle-working power of the Lord. And in this way, anyone could recognize the Son of David and true Shepherd of Israel. Therefore, is it any surprise that Nicodemus, the educated Torah scholar and Pharisee, comes to Jesus saying, "We know that you are a teacher come from God, for no one can do these signs that you do unless God is with him" (John 3:2)?

A Message to the Enemies of God

Finally, David makes a bold promise to Goliath, one that is packed with prophecy: to "cut off [his] head" (1 Sam 17:46). The cutting or crushing of the head is popular biblical imagery that not only feeds us future information about the profile of the Messiah, but this brief flash of four words takes us back through time and history all the way to Gen 3 where it originated.

Perhaps you already guessed it, but this imagery reminds the reader of the famous, prophetic words God delivers to the serpent in Gen 3:15 just after the fall of humankind: "I will put enmity between you and the woman, and between your offspring and hers; *he will crush your head*, and you will strike his heel."

Scholars describe Gen 3:15 as the first hint or "announcement" of the gospel[13]—in seed-like form. In other words, it is the gospel's very first ripple. The promise of an offspring belonging to the woman and who will crush the head of God's enemies begins a ripple effect within Israel's history. David is not the first to partially fulfill and prophetically foreshadow this "head-crushing" business on the enemies of God's people, although it

13. Carson, "Fall."

does climax drastically in him as God's chosen messiah in 1 Sam 17. But we glimpse this prophetic ripple in other stories of Israel long before David.

A Head-Crushing Wife Who Can Find?

Interestingly, in many other places where we see this "head-crushing" imagery in the Bible, it is women who are doing it. Or, if they are not themselves performing it, they are involved in a very central and indispensable way like Eve, whose head-crushing offspring is intentionally described as belonging to and coming from *her* ("her offspring," as opposed to the far more common biblical emphasis on patriarchal lineage/seed). Perhaps the most famous of these head-crushing women is Jael in the times of the Judges:

> Most blessed of women be Jael,
> the wife of Heber the Kenite,
> most blessed of tent-dwelling women....
> Her hand reached for the tent peg,
> her right hand for the workman's hammer.
> She struck Sisera, she *crushed his head*,
> she *shattered* and *pierced his temple*. (Judg 5:24, 26 NIV)

The same event is also recorded in Judg 4:21 where, "Jael, Heber's wife, picked up a tent peg and a hammer and went quietly to him while he lay fast asleep, exhausted. She drove the peg through his *temple* into the ground, and he died" (NIV).

In Judg 9:52–53, we see a similar picture of a certain unnamed woman who drops an upper millstone on the head of King Abimelek, thus crushing his head: "Abimelek went to the tower and attacked it. But as he approached the entrance to the tower to set it on fire, a woman dropped an upper *millstone* on *his head* and *cracked his skull*" (NIV). Interestingly, David also throws a stone that "sank into [Goliath's] forehead" (1 Sam 17:49).

Although it is found in extrabiblical literature, the story of Judith is again another victory won for Israel by a woman. Judith is said to have beheaded the Assyrian general Holofernes with his own sword (Jdt 12–13) just as David beheaded Goliath with Goliath's own sword (1 Sam 17:41–58).

The women of the Bible are quite dangerous. Whether physical or spiritual warriors, they are often Israel's secret weapons, like hidden snipers. And where they are mentioned, they succeed immensely in bringing down God's enemies. And this is the main point behind the head-crushing imagery of the Bible. The song about Jael concludes with the key words, "So may all your enemies perish, Lord! Then the land had peace forty years" (Judg 5:31 NIV). This head-crushing imagery is always paired with the fight against God's enemies, and as a result, God's people would experience peace.

While peace is not the immediate result in 1 Sam 17, 1 Sam 18:14 says David had success wherever he went and against whomever he fought, thus establishing a new kind of security throughout the land that the people hadn't experienced under Saul. Later, after becoming king, 2 Sam 7:1 says the Lord gave David "rest from all his surrounding enemies" (2 Sam 7:1). One of the main tasks of God's messiah and king was to save God's people from their enemies and secure peace.

Significantly, the above women are repeatedly praised and called "blessed" for crushing Israel's enemies. "Most blessed of women be Jael" (Judg 5:24). "Then Uzziah said to her, 'O daughter, you are blessed by the Most High God above all other women on earth, and blessed be the Lord God, who created the heavens and the earth, who has guided you to cut off the head of the leader of our enemies'" (Jdt 13:18 NRSVUE).

These "blessed" women and this head-crushing imagery all develop and grow to ultimately foreshadow and find fulfillment in the truly most blessed of women: Mary, the mother of Jesus. The praises given to the above women align with the familiar praise Elizabeth gives to Jesus' mother: "Blessed are you among women, and blessed is the fruit of your womb!" (Luke 1:42). She is blessed because in her, the ancient, head-crushing prophecy of Gen 3:15 will be fulfilled. Her offspring will be the ultimate seed who will crush the ultimate enemy of God and save his people.

You see, Mary is the new Eve or the better Eve. She is the most developed ripple of a woman participating in God's head-crushing business. Jesus, *her* offspring, is the second or last Adam as Paul says in 1 Cor 15:45–49. Salvation and the head-crushing seed came into the world through Mary who stands in redeeming contrast to Eve. Just as Eve brought sin and death into the world by obeying the serpent, Mary birthed salvation into the world, the messianic defeat of sin, Satan, and death. And he will usher in *everlasting* peace, eternal shalom to all Israel and into all the world. Indeed, a head-crushing wife who can find? She is worth far more than rubies.

So with this flashback to Gen 3:15 embedded within 1 Sam 17—David's cutting off Goliath's head—we ought to understand that God is not only continuing the ancient prophecy of the head-crushing seed through David and his line, but that the Seed of the woman and the Son of David will be one and the same. Crushing God's enemies becomes the messianic pattern for what the future Messiah will do as both the Seed of the woman and Son of David.

And by his victory, the knowledge of the God of Israel will spread to all nations, and peace will finally permeate the land. But the peace Messiah ushers in will be far better than the temporary peace David brought. The peace the Seed of the woman inaugurates will in fact be a restoration of the perfect paradise that was lost in Eden and a reversal of that curse. And that is what Jesus, the Prince of Peace, began with his first arrival when he initiated the coming of his kingdom. He brings peace from the inside out, touching lives and transforming people from within. Later, he will bring full peace on earth when he returns to usher in the fullness of his messianic kingdom.

Finally, the apostle Paul, who surely knew his Jewish history, picks up the ripple of the offspring who crushes the head of the serpent (and everything we discussed) and recycles it for believers who are in Jesus, saying, "The God of *peace* will soon *crush Satan under your feet*" (Rom 16:20). As the head of Goliath lay at David's feet (and by extension Israel's feet), so the Son of David has put the enemy of our soul under the believer's feet.

Do you know this peace?

Chapter Esther[1]

> For we are a fragrance of Christ to God among those who are being saved and among those who are perishing: to the one an aroma from death to death, to the other an aroma from life to life. —2 Corinthians 2:15–16, NASB

MANY WOMEN IN THE Bible are marvelous heroes who not only evoke God's image in their day but also receive the privilege of imaging the Messiah himself. Esther is one of them. God includes Esther and her story in the line of great biblical heroes who serve as a foreshadowing fragrance of the Messiah and his story.

One of the first things we observe about the book of Esther is that God's name is never directly mentioned. In fact, God is not identified or brought up at all. This does not mean God is not active or that this book is not Scripture; rather, it simply gives us a different and indirect window into viewing God's activity and character, one that exercises faith—which, in one sense, is what this book is all about.

So while God may remain hidden, he is surely present. In the book of Esther, God is to be found in and through *his people*. And when we consider Esther herself, we are overwhelmed with characteristic signs of God's mighty hand at work.

---

1. Much of the following content comes from an article I wrote in an eBook: "Lessons from Esther," 24–27.

Chapter Esther

DIVINE FAVOR IN THE BOOK OF ESTHER

God's favor rests upon Esther in such conspicuous ways—ways that in fact serve as flashbacks to other biblical people whom God raised up and used for special purposes, people like Joseph and Daniel, who also experienced the Lord's favor for divine (and messianic) purposes. But not only will Esther echo biblical figures from the past, she will foreshadow the future Messiah himself, as we shall see.

God's presence can be spotted by the way he is powerfully with Esther, continuously giving her immense favor in everybody's eyes from the beginning to the end of the story. And I mean *continuously*, beginning with the strong relationship she has with her cousin, Mordechai, who "took her as his own daughter" when her parents died (Esth 2:7). From there,

1. Esther receives favor in the eyes of the eunuch who was in charge of the harem (2:9) and then in the eyes of the king himself so that she becomes queen of Persia (2:17).

2. An often overlooked detail is that Esther even has favor in the eyes of Haman himself, which not even Mordechai possessed (5:12). And this favor in her enemy's eyes plays a providential part in causing Haman's downfall.

3. It is colossal favor that causes the king to extend his scepter to Esther when she transgresses the law of approaching the king without being summoned (5:2).

4. It was great, divine favor that moves the king to heed the voice of Esther, a woman and a Jew, over his highest favored, male advisor, Haman (Esther 7).

5. In the end, the king gives Esther and Mordechai free reign to write and seal another edict counteracting the edict that he had granted Haman (8:8). Truly, "the king's heart is a stream of water in the hand of the Lord; he turns it wherever he will" (Prov 21:1).

Such persistent favor is neither coincidence nor random luck; it can only proceed from God. Also, this kind of divine favor was not new or unique to Esther, and I'm on the side of believing both Mordechai and Esther were aware of God's hand moving around and within them. After all, they would have recognized the ripples of this divine favor in their people's history: it was the same favor of God's presence that followed Daniel into exile, giving him wisdom above and beyond all the other wise men (Dan 1:17–20, 2:46–48, 5:13–16, 6:3). It was also this same favor that raised Joseph from slavery and prison to be the second highest in command over all of Egypt (Gen 41:38–41). And of course, we can go on and on. There's always a divine agenda behind such considerable favor causing highly improbable and unlikely events. Esther's favor reveals God's quite obvious presence, despite his hiddenness. Additionally, this divine favor, like in Joseph's story (Gen 45:5–7), results in the saving of God's people!

Now, it must be said that divine favor does not remove trials, nor does it promise comfort. Just like Joseph and Daniel experienced setbacks and suffering despite God's favor in their lives, Esther too encounters difficulties, fears, and risks—including the risk of death (Esth 4:11). I believe there's enough evidence in Esther 4 to infer that Esther experiences hesitation, anxiety, and the very real and human temptation toward self-preservation. Perhaps she desired to be silent instead of speaking out, or perhaps she even confused silence with submission—which many women do!

Yet, whatever her inner conflict was, Esther stands as an example to us all, male and female, as we see her overcome very real and human struggles and choose to perform the will of the Lord, even to the point of potentially perishing (Esth 4:16).

Also, let us not overlook the fact that Esther becomes more confident and spiritually strengthened for her destined mission only *after* she calls for communal fasting and seeking the Lord (Esth 4:16). Additionally, Esther surrounds herself with godly counsel and trustworthy voices in tune to God's will like Mordechai. His advice not only forever altered the course of Esther's life, but it saved lives!

MESSIANIC PARALLELS: ESTHER AND JESUS

Finally, God includes Esther in the line of great biblical heroes who had the highest privilege of foreshadowing the Messiah himself. Although centuries apart, Esther and Jesus share much in common! It's almost as if they have a similar heart, a similar spirit, and even similar words. Let's look at some texts.

Chapter Esther

Divine Favor

Firstly, the divine favor that rippled through the lives of Joseph, Daniel, Esther, and so many others within the Bible culminates in Jesus, who experienced "favor with God and man" (Luke 2:52). We see God's favor at work in Jesus as he teaches with authority, unlike the scribes and teachers of the law (Matt 7:29). We also know that all his miracles were prayers favorably answered from above, even the raising from the dead. After resurrecting Lazarus, "Jesus lifted up his eyes and said, 'Father, I thank you that you have heard me. I knew that you always hear me'" (John 11:41–42). Lastly, like Joseph and Esther, the divine favor that rested upon Jesus resulted in a great salvation—of both Jews and gentiles.

Seeking Support

Next, we see Esther ask for support by inviting the Jewish community and her young women to fast with her before going to the king at the risk of death. Esther 4:16 says, "Go, gather all the Jews to be found in Susa, and hold a fast on my behalf, and do not eat or drink for three days, night or day. I and my young women will also fast."

Likewise, Jesus invited his disciples to support and keep watch with him in the garden of Gethsemane just before going to the Sanhedrin and Pilate at the risk—or guarantee—of death. Matthew 26:38 says, "[Jesus] said to them, 'My soul is overwhelmed with sorrow to the point of death. Stay here and keep watch with me.'" In their last hour, Esther and Jesus both wrestle with the looming threat of death, seek the Lord, and request the support of others.

Willingness to Die

Significantly, we observe both Esther and Jesus sharing a courageous willingness to die for their people out of profound love and submission to God's will. After wrestling and praying and fasting, they both arrive at a new strengthened posture that enables them to *choose* courage and sacrificial love in the face of death. Esther's famous words "If I perish, I perish" (4:16) bear a strange semblance to Jesus' own blood-sweating words: "Not as I will, but as You will" (Matt 26:39). Both deeply internalize the unavoidable reality of facing death and reach the same resolve: *your will be done* (Matt

6:10). Indeed, both Esther and Jesus could say with confidence, "No one takes [my life] from me, but I lay it down of my own accord" (John 10:18).

Intercessors Between Life and Death

Finally, Esther and Jesus both function as mediators interceding between life and death for their people. Esther 8:3 says, "[Esther] fell at [the king's] feet and wept and pleaded with him to avert the evil plan of Haman the Agagite and the plot that he had devised against the Jews." Romans 8:34 says, "Christ Jesus is the one who died—more than that, who was raised—who is at the right hand of God, who indeed is interceding for us."

And if you haven't already noticed, both Esther's and Jesus' intercession succeeds in changing or canceling the edict that stood against God's people condemning them to death. Esther 8:8 records the king granting Esther and Mordechai the equivalent of a blank check to write a new edict "as [they] please with regard to the Jews, in the name of the king, and seal it with the king's ring, for an edict written in the name of the king and sealed with the king's ring cannot be revoked."

And regarding Jesus, Col 2:13–14 says he forgave us all our trespasses "by *canceling the record* of debt that stood against us with its legal demands. This he set aside, nailing it to the cross." Interestingly, the very next verse bears a striking resemblance to what happened to Haman: "And having disarmed the powers and authorities, he made a public spectacle of them, triumphing over them by the cross" (Col 2:15 NIV). Not only was Haman disarmed, but he died publicly on the very gallows he had built for Mordechai (Esth 7:10), who emerged triumphant in his fight against Haman.

To be sure, Jesus' intercession is greater in that it actually revoked and canceled the edict condemning us to death. Nevertheless, Esther's story is a major foreshadowing of the gospel story and Jesus' intercession. Her story serves as a prophetic ripple moving toward a better intercessor and a bigger salvation. The Messiah comes sharing in her experience, and his story would even be patterned upon her own.

If you think about it, Hadassah (Esther's Hebrew name) emptied herself of all the familiar comforts of her people, taking on the form of a slave in the king's harem. Going from Hadassah to Esther was a major humbling and, in many ways for her, death. She would experience perpetual separation from Mordechai and her people, the denial of her Jewish identity and heritage, and the scandal of identifying with the corrupt ways of the

Chapter Esther

Persians especially as a concubine. But, like Joseph, she rose up in rank, and as queen, she quite literally sat at the right hand of the king. That position and the immense favor she experienced in the sight of the king enabled her to intercede for her people and succeed.

We know that Jesus—though he existed in the form of God—emptied himself of the glories of heaven and gave up his divine privileges, not counting "equality with God a thing to be grasped" (Phil 2:6). He took on the humble position of a slave (Phil 2:7) and took upon himself all our corrupt ways and sins. Jesus had immense favor with God all throughout his life, and even in his death, his sacrifice pleased God so that he rose from the dead and took a seat at the right hand of God where he now effectively intercedes for us. "Christ Jesus is the one who died—more than that, who was raised—who is at the right hand of God, who indeed is interceding for us" (Rom 8:34).

This picture of the Messiah dying, rising again, and sitting at the right hand of God is not strictly a New Testament idea. As we've seen, this pattern is uniquely sown and developed in the lives and stories of many of God's people before Jesus stepped onto the scene (like Joseph). Even national Israel's exiles and destruction always came with the hope of restoration and, in the strong messianic language and imagery of Ezekiel, the *resurrection* of both the land and the people (Ezek 36:8–12, 35; 37:11–14).

Perhaps this is why we observe an exasperated Jesus saying to the disciples on the road to Emmaus: "O foolish ones, and slow of heart to believe all that the prophets have spoken! Was it not necessary that the Christ should suffer these things and enter into his glory?" (Luke 24:25–26). The pattern was always there, rippling through both the stories of Israel and the prophets.

In summary, it is the hidden spirit of Jesus that moves in the events of the book of Esther and within Esther herself to pave the messianic path of selfless sacrifice. Esther truly was "a fragrance of Christ among those who are being saved [her people] and among those who are perishing [Haman]. To the one an aroma from death to death, to the other an aroma from life to life" (2 Cor 2:15–16).

I conclude this first section in chapter Esther with a brief encouragement on the themes we just examined. Though God might seem hidden in your circumstances, he is in fact very present, working behind the scenes of your life out of a profound, selfless love. When you know in your innermost being that you have such a self-sacrificing mediator fighting for your life and taking your death, you can follow him into the riskiest and scariest situations of life—or death. And even if we perish, we perish unto resurrection and everlasting life with our Messiah.

THE GENIUS OF IRONY IN THE BOOK OF ESTHER

This section will shift from tracing story ripples to explore another equally beloved literary device in the Bible: irony. The world of literature classifies irony in three basic categories: dramatic, verbal, and situational irony.[2] But at the heart of all irony is a "contradiction of our perceived reality" or "a contrast between "what seems to be" and "what is.""[3] And the form we will explore in this section is situational irony, which is experiencing the reverse or contrary of what was expected. Situational irony permeates Scripture, but perhaps the book that takes the gold in irony is the book of Esther. Moreover, irony serves as one of the biggest clues to detecting God's hand and activity in the book of Esther.

God's active presence is best detected through the ironic switching up of lots, or *pûr* in Hebrew. As with the entire book of Esther, this word is very ironic and fitting given the storyline. Esther 9:24 records that Haman "cast *pûr* [that is, cast lots]" to annihilate the Jewish people. But by the end of the book, it is clear God has a different lot for the Jews—and for Haman. The irony is that he switches the lots. Haman and his people are destroyed (the very lot he intended for the Jewish people) while the Jewish community, Esther, and Mordechai are not only delivered but the latter two rise in rank to possess Haman's own position and favor. So, in biblical language, Haman's intentions for Mordechai and the Jews return upon his own head and household.[4]

---

2. Dramatic irony is "when the audience knows something the story's characters do not, resulting in poor decision making or ironic consequences" (Glatch, "Irony Definition"). It is that moment you begin yelling at the TV because Romeo is about to kill himself thinking his Juliet is already dead, when *you* in fact know she is merely sleeping. Verbal irony is "an instance of dialogue where one thing is spoken, but a contrasting meaning is intended" (Glatch, "Irony Definition"). It's when you wake up, pull the curtains, and say "What a glorious day! Perfect for the park!" even though there is a blizzard raging outside your window. Situational irony is "when a certain event or reaction is expected, and an entirely contradictory one occurs (Glatch, "Irony Definition"). It's the ironic twist of Joseph forgiving and even saving his brothers who sold him into slavery (Gen 50:20).

3. Glatch, "Irony Definition."

4. See Ps 7:16; Joel 3:7; Obad 1:15; Prov 11:5–6, 26:27.

Chapter Esther

Haman and Mordechai

Irony is the defining feature characterizing Haman's relationship and competition with Mordechai. And as we investigate the irony at work between these two men, we detect God's fingerprints everywhere:

1. Haman is forced to parade and honor Mordechai around town according to the exact description Haman suggested to the king (thinking it was for himself) (Esth 6:6–10).
2. Haman is made to honor Mordechai while Mordechai never once bows to Haman (Esth 3:2–4; 5:9; 6:11).
3. Haman's promotion at the beginning of the story is given to Mordechai at the end of the story (Esth 3:1; 8:1–2).
4. Haman is hanged on the gallows he intended for Mordechai (Esth 7:9–10).
5. Haman's plot to destroy all of the Jews because of Mordechai (Esth 3:5–6) is pronounced over Haman's ten sons because of Haman (Esth 9:13–14).

If you know your Bible well, you know that this kind of irony is very characteristic of God. Likewise, I believe Mordechai knew God was not only present throughout these events but that he was proactively fighting for his people with his favorite weapon: irony. And I dare say Mordechai even knew that Haman stood no chance in messing with God's people because Mordechai knew his Scriptures well, especially those verses detailing the inescapability of God's mysteriously ironic ways:

1. "He frustrates the devices of the crafty, so that their hands achieve no success. He catches the wise in their own craftiness, and the schemes of the wily are brought to a quick end" (Job 5:12–13).
2. "Truly you set [the wicked] in slippery places; you make them fall to ruin. How they are destroyed in a moment, swept away utterly by terrors!" (Ps 73:18–19).
3. "Pride goes before destruction, and a haughty spirit before a fall" (Prov 16:18).
4. "I will bless those who bless you, and whoever curses you I will curse" (Gen 12:3 NIV).

5. "One's pride will bring him low, but he who is lowly in spirit will obtain honor" (Prov 29:23).

6. "Be still before the Lord and wait patiently for him; fret not yourself over the one who prospers in his way, over the man who carries out evil devices!" (Ps 37:7).

7. "The Lord is my chosen portion and my cup; *you* hold my *lot*. The lines have fallen for me in *pleasant* places" (Ps 16:5–6).

8. "The king's heart is a stream of water in the hand of the Lord; he turns it wherever he will" (Prov 21:1).

It isn't only the Scriptures that reveal God's ironic ways, but the very literary structure of the entire book of Esther is itself a witness that magnifies this irony and showcases God's hidden genius.

Literary Structure of the Book of Esther

While scholars discuss multiple worthy angles for structuring the events in the book of Esther, I have listed below one of the more well-known and fascinating examples. It incorporates a literary device highly favored by the biblical writers called chiasm, a form of inverse parallelism where the beginning and end of the book mirror each other with important accentuation upon the center. The center of a chiasm is usually the place where the author is drawing attention, establishing emphasis, or unfolding a pivotal turn of events. Chiasm is similar to irony in that it is a sort of play on opposites in order to make a point or spotlight a point. An example is always more helpful, so here is one of the chiastic literary structures of the book of Esther:

CHAPTER ESTHER

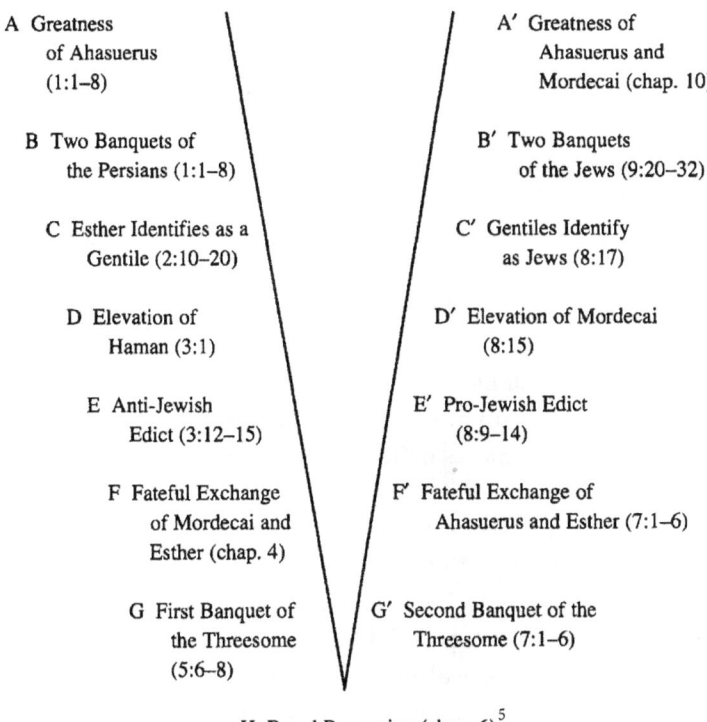

H Royal Procession (chap. 6)[5]

You can see that at the center of the story is the royal procession of Mordechai by Haman. Up until this point in chapter 6, Haman has been the one honored and promoted while Mordechai was humbled and lowered even to the point of sackcloth and ashes because of the anti-Jewish edict (Esth 4:1). But in chapter 6, the storyline pivots and the tables begin to turn, like a game of chess. Chapter 6 is being spotlighted because this is the turning point, the beginning of Haman's downfall and the beginning of Mordechai's rise. And as their lots switch, so does the lot of Mordechai's people and Haman's house. It is a genius work of irony.

The Gospel as a Genius Work of Irony

In the book of Esther, it is clear how God works through irony to bring about the salvation of his people. But did you know God also used irony to bring about the salvation of the whole world? Indeed, biblical salvation

---

5. Levenson, *Esther*, 8. Used by permission of Westminster John Knox Press (WJKP).

is itself a work of irony. The same irony that permeates the book of Esther ripples into the gospel story.

In Jesus, God actively switches the lot of sinners. Let me explain with an example. Isaiah 53 describes an innocent servant who has himself done no wrong but who bears the sin of others and is numbered as with transgressors (9, 12). He also makes "a guilt offering," and by that offering, "many are accounted righteous" (10–11). In other words, Jesus receives the lot of our guilt, sin, and sicknesses and we bear the lot of his innocence, righteousness, and healing. In Jesus, God exchanges lots, and by doing so, brings salvation and life to people doomed under the unalterable edict of death; his death for our life.

You may have heard of the gospel described as "the great exchange," but this exchange also makes it the greatest irony in history. Who wouldn't make the eternal trade?

Just as we saw in the book of Esther, God switches lots in the gospel story in very hidden ways. Where it seems like Jesus is losing, he is actually winning.[6] In losing his life, he is cancelling our death. In crying out, "My God why have you forsaken me?", Jesus is securing our eternal belonging to the degree that nothing will ever separate us from the love of God (Rom 8:35–39) or snatch us out of our Shepherd's hands (John 10:28).

G. K. Beale points out, "The very thing that Satan thought would destroy Christ and give Satan the victory—is itself a defeat for Satan. He's hung on his own gallows."[7] Just as Haman sought to put Mordechai to death, so Satan sought to kill Jesus by crucifixion. "And yet, just as Haman was hung on his own gallows, the devil himself was hung on his own gallows. At the cross, Jesus is taking the penalty of sin for sinners who've been in captivity to Satan."[8] In dying on the cross, Jesus is ironically cancelling the edict of death Satan held in his hands.

Finally, on the day of judgment/resurrection, God will finally complete all the switches. He will set all wrongs right. Curses will turn to blessings. Injustice will give way to justice, death to life, disorder to order, sickness to health, tears to laughter, and so on. Even enemies will turn into family. So many—if not all—of God's judgments will incorporate this ancient irony. Therefore, as in the book of Esther, it is of utmost importance that

---

6. Beale, "Greatest Example of Irony in the Bible."
7. Beale, "Greatest Example of Irony in the Bible."
8. Beale, "Greatest Example of Irony in the Bible."

every soul finds him/herself on the side of God's people and their successful intercessor.

Questions for Reflection—and Action!

1. Have you allowed Jesus to cancel the legal edict standing against you, condemning you to eternal death? Have you made the grand switch Jesus freely offers? Your guilt for his righteousness. Your sicknesses for his healing. Your death for his abundant life—both now and forevermore. Switch your lot, friend, for "he is able to save completely those who come to God through him, because he always lives to intercede for them" (Heb 7:25).

2. Where do you observe Haman's spirit and attitude being relived and recycled in the history of antisemitism? What lessons and action steps can believers glean from the efforts and example of Mordechai and Esther for combatting this oldest and cosmic hatred in our present day?

Conclusion

MAVERICK CITY MUSIC AND UPPERROOM have a popular song entitled "I Thank God" that sings the Bible verse, "The testimony of Jesus is the spirit of prophecy" (Rev 19:10), and then interprets it in a way that summarizes this entire book in a few simple words:

> That means what he did for another, he can do it again.[1]

Indeed, this is how we've seen prophecy work in the Bible. What God has done in the past, he does it again and again in more lives and more stories. The prophetic patterns ripple onward—toward Messiah and those united to him forever.

If you listen closely, most Christian worship songs have story ripples as their foundation. The lyrics invite you into worship through a Spirit-led recycling of Bible stories, themes, and patterns to your life and soul. Take, for example, the lyrics to "No Longer Slaves":

> I'm no longer a slave to fear; I am a child of God.
> You split the sea so I could walk right through it.
> My fears were drowned in perfect love.
> You rescued me and I will stand and sing, "I am a child of God."[2]

These lyrics are a flashback to the original exodus story—Israel's slavery in Egypt and their experience of God's mighty rescue, especially in the parting of the Red Sea. But the songwriter is taking this same story with its sea-splitting imagery and recasting it to describe how God works redemption in our souls today. The artist is using the power of story in the Bible—and its ripple effect.[3]

1. Chiriboga et al., "I Thank God."
2. Helser et al., "No Longer Slaves."
3. This point assumes that such reapplication is done correctly, remains biblical,

Conclusion

While it can and certainly has been abused, the recycling of biblical stories remains the gateway to experiencing the transcending, enduring word of God that will never pass away (Isa 40:8; Matt 24:35).[4] We know that everything "written in former days was written for our instruction" (Rom 15:4). The story ripples of the Bible open a portal between heaven and earth for the soul to encounter the life-giving power of God's words, to be entirely transformed, to be infused with purpose and perspective, to hear God's voice, to enjoy his real presence, and to enter into soul-satisfying worship.

These divinely-inspired stories live on, supernaturally causing people in the future to join God's story and identify with the events of Scripture to an important extent. Sometimes, that extent is a matter of much-needed encouragement; other times, it's a matter of eternal life or death! Encountering the words of God in the Bible is real *soul work* that saves and changes lives forever. It's the mysterious work and power we experience in anointed sermons where the words of God ripple from the text into our souls. What God did in the past, he works it again in the present; and you can expect him to do it yet again in the future.

---

and does not add to or subtract from the word of God. This can be a fine line to balance, but the important thing that needs to be said here is that it is the Holy Spirit who leads and works biblical ripples into our lives; it is he who uses and recasts the words of God to speak to our souls. Insofar as he is leading and inspiring the use of such imagery, themes, patterns, and stories from the Bible, we can rest assured that our impressions and experiences remain within biblical boundaries. Always treat text as the literature it is before seeking to draw out spiritual import into your life. Never rush or force meaning onto a text. Let the Spirit of God take his time to develop a ripple or theme into your life on *his* terms.

4. An example of an abuse of the wonder of story ripples is the doctrine of replacement theology (also known as supersessionism). This false doctrine is rooted in a sweeping reinterpretation of biblical texts that proposes Christians have replaced Jewish people as the chosen people of God and that all the promises in the Bible that originally were meant for Israel are now transferred over to believers in Jesus only. In other words, instead of *sharing* into Israel's stories and experiences, supersessionism *steals* those stories. This is not a mere reapplication but an entire rereading of the Bible, one that is to be wholeheartedly rejected because it severs and scraps the original and previous meanings of biblical texts and replaces them with another meaning. It doesn't allow for the literary ripple effect among Bible stories. Additionally, replacement theology does not align with other biblical truths, such as: 1) God's eternal and unbreakable covenant with the people of Israel (1 Chr 16:14–18; Jer 31:36–37); 2) the fact that God never rejected his people, which is made very clear to us by the apostle Paul in Rom 11; and 3) the clear concept that gentile believers are grafted into Israel's olive tree (Rom 11:17). In Jesus, gentiles are welcomed to share in the story, not steal it as their own. As with everything else, we need to allow *all* Scripture to be our guide in the handling and experience of God's word.

The Story Ripples of the Bible

This is the genius of story in the Bible (and the storyteller). There is no other book out there that so pulls its readers in as participants. In the Bible, we get invited by God into his adventures. "Rule number one for reading the stories of the Bible is simply this: *look upon biblical stories as an invitation to share an experience, as vividly and concretely as possible, with the characters in the story.*"[5] The stories and experiences of Bible characters not only come together in Jesus who fulfilled them uniquely and singularly, but they also get recycled and *re*-presented in those who become united with the Messiah and, therefore, the stories of all Israel.

We are meant to share in Israel's experiences. Their stories become testimonies living, breathing, and working in your soul by the power of the Holy Spirit. "For the word of God is living and active, sharper than any two-edged sword, piercing to the division of soul and of spirit, of joints and of marrow, and discerning the thoughts and intentions of the heart" (Heb 4:12).

Especially with the ancient pattern of death and resurrection—this ripple is now what all believers are baptized into:

> Do you not know that all of us who have been baptized into Christ Jesus were baptized into his death? We were buried therefore with him by baptism into death, in order that, just as Christ was raised from the dead by the glory of the Father, we too might walk in newness of life. For if we have been united with him in a death like his, we shall certainly be united with him in a resurrection like his. (Rom 6:3–5)

You, too, were meant to be restored into God's garden-paradise and walk in newness of life. You were destined to be a character in God's story, walking in the footsteps and sharing the faith of those who have gone before us. You may feel like a nobody who has nothing, but as you read about God's people in his many stories, you see that is exactly who God chooses and how most of the major biblical characters began their stories: Abraham, Moses, Israel as a nation, David, Hannah, Nehemiah, the disciples—and even Jesus, who humbled himself to the status of a mere carpenter's son without position, wealth, or prestige.

Come join the adventure of life. Enter into God's ripple effect through the Messiah, toward whom all stories move. Stop trying to write your own life story; it's not going to be half as good or abundant as what the Author of Life can write for you. Relinquish the pen. Join in the ancient stories that

---

5. Ryken, *How to Read the Bible*, 34–35.

Conclusion

the Ancient of Days has been writing and is still writing. As he used others in the past to tell his story and fulfill his plans, he is still using people today to continue writing the last chapters. And he wants to use *you*.

If you are already united to the Messiah, take time to think over your story, your testimony, your life experiences. Contemplate their "prophetic" nature—how you have come to share in the stories of long ago. After all, the same Spirit that moved in the people of the past and authored their stories is the same Spirit now living in *you* (Rom 8:11). No need to daydream about time traveling in the Bible because God has already plugged you into his story and destined you to experience the Bible's many ripples.

Which Bible stories do you resonate with? Are you aware of biblical themes, patterns, and ripples at work in your life? Which of these forerunners, forefathers, and great females of the faith has God used to speak to your soul and shape your story?

Perhaps you, too, were called by God to leave everything behind and go to an unfamiliar place. If so, then Abraham is your guy. Study and glean from his story. Perhaps you've been woefully wronged and are forced to process immense injustice and agonizing abuse even from the hands of those closest to you. Joseph has much say. Notice how God reserved pages and chapters in his best-selling book to record Joseph's story, his raw emotions, and his long journey back to reconciliation. David, too, God's chosen and anointed king, suffered lengthy injustice at the hunting hands of Saul, even to the point of being driven from his share in the Lord's inheritance (1 Sam 26:19).

Of all people, David also learned what it meant to be adopted and loved by the Lord due to his father and mother forsaking him (Ps 27:10). Perhaps you've been barren for the longest time. Come take your pick out of the long line of women and matriarchs who wrestled with God in very different ways. Maybe you find yourself in a leadership position you didn't ask for or that is too heavy for your shoulders. Moses understood this deeply. Learn how to put up with difficult people from him. Even he took much needed advice to lighten his burden (Exod 18:13-27). Learn from his costly mistakes (Deut 4:21). Most importantly, follow his example of making generous space for deep intimacy with the Lord (Exod 34:28-29).

Spend time walking with God through his words, his ripples, his people, and his Messiah. Especially when life around you crumbles and you feel yourself coming apart, clinging to this supernatural book with its transcending story ripples will prove a lifeline and breakthrough. You will discover what author Esther Fleece Allen has said so well even as she feared for her own life: "[My Bible] is the only thing that gets me."[6]

Brothers and sisters, you have been united to the greatest stories ever told, stories that are carried on in you and that also carry you. The Bible is replete with themes and perspectives God intends to work in you and through you. That alone is incredibly helpful to know as you walk through this life. When we abide in Jesus—in his words, in these stories—we become used by God like our forefathers and foremothers of the faith. We bear fruit and propagate the promises. He uses our stories to continue his story.

Most importantly, to study these stories is to know Jesus more deeply, more intimately—and to know your new identity more fully. For you will walk where Jesus walked. United to him forever, you are destined to share his story in every way—both the way of the cross and of imperishable glory.

For you have died, and your life is hidden with the Messiah in God. When the Messiah, who is your life, is revealed, then you also will be revealed with Him in glory. —Colossians 3:3–4, HCSB

---

6. Fleece, *I Am Second*. Esther's books are *No More Faking Fine* and *Your New Name* (which she wrote as Esther Fleece Allen).

Bibliography

Allen, Esther Fleece. *Your New Name: Saying Goodbye to the Labels That Limit You.* Grand Rapids: Zondervan, 2020.
Amzallag, Nissim. "Beyond Idolatry: The Transgression of the Golden Calf Revisited." *Old Testament Essays* 33 (2020) 207–31.
Ancient Egypt Online. "Hathor." https://ancientegyptonline.co.uk/hathor/.
Baldwin, Joyce G. *1 and 2 Samuel: An Introduction and Commentary.* Tyndale Old Testament Commentaries 8. Downers Grove, IL: InterVarsity, 1988.
Barry, John D., et al. *Faithlife Study Bible.* Bellingham, WA: Lexham, 2016. Accessed via Logos Bible Software.
Beale, G. K. "The Greatest Example of Irony in the Bible." Crossway, Nov. 14, 2019. https://www.crossway.org/articles/the-greatest-example-of-irony-in-the-bible/.
Bible Hub. "393. anatellō." https://biblehub.com/greek/393.htm.
———. "395. anatolē." https://biblehub.com/greek/395.htm.
———. "4637. skēnoō." https://biblehub.com/greek/4637.htm.
———. "John 1:14." https://biblehub.com/john/1-14.htm.
Bock, Darrell L. "Quests for the Historical Jesus." The Gospel Coalition. https://www.thegospelcoalition.org/essay/quests-historical-jesus/.
Britannica. "11 Egyptian Gods and Goddesses." https://www.britannica.com/list/11-egyptian-gods-and-goddesses.
———. "The Gods." https://www.britannica.com/topic/ancient-Egyptian-religion/The-Gods.
———. "Hathor." https://www.britannica.com/topic/Hathor-Egyptian-goddess.
Carroll, Lewis. *Alice's Adventures in Wonderland.* New York: Dover, 1993.
Carson, Don. "The Fall (Part 1)." The Gospel Coalition. https://www.thegospelcoalition.org/sermon/part-1-the-fall-genesis-3/.
Chase, Mitchell L. *40 Questions About Typology and Allegory.* Edited by Benjamin L. Merkle. Grand Rapids: Kregel Academic, 2020.
Chiriboga, Aaron Moses, et al. "I Thank God." *Move Your Heart.* Track 7. 2020.
Chosen People Ministries. "Presenting Messiah to Your Jewish Friend." https://chosenpeople.com/presenting-messiah-to-your-jewish-friend/.
Coogan, Michael David. *The Old Testament: A Historical and Literary Introduction to the Hebrew Scriptures.* New York: Oxford University Press, 2013.
Cook, William F. "Who Are the Sons of God in Genesis 6?" The Gospel Coalition, Jan. 6, 2020. https://www.thegospelcoalition.org/article/who-are-sons-of-god-genesis-6/.

Bibliography

"Desert." *Logos Bible Study Factbook*. Bellingham, WA: Faithlife, LLC. https://ref.ly/logos4/Factbook?id=ref%3abk.%25desert.

Diamant, Anita. "The Huppah (Chuppah): What You Need to Know." *My Jewish Learning*. Accessed May 30, 2025. https://www.myjewishlearning.com/article/chuppah/.

Eames, Christopher. "Evidence for Worship of the Golden Calf?" Armstrong Institute of Biblical Archeology. https://armstronginstitute.org/235-evidence-for-worship-of-the-golden-calf?.

"The Exodus: Fact or Fiction?" Biblical Archaeology Society. https://www.biblicalarchaeology.org/daily/biblical-topics/exodus/exodus-fact-or-fiction/.

Fausset, A. R. *A Commentary, Critical, Experimental, and Practical, on the Old and New Testaments: Job–Isaiah*. Glasgow: William Collins, 1864.

Fleece, Esther. "I Am Second." Video, Excerpt (9:17). https://www.iamsecond.com/film/esther-fleece-allen/#modal-media-vimeo.

———. *No More Faking Fine: Ending the Pretending*. Grand Rapids: Zondervan, 2017.

Frost, Robert. "Education by Poetry." In *Robert Frost: Collected Poems, Prose, and Plays*, edited by Richard Poirier and Mark Richardson, 717–28. New York: The Library of America, 1995.

Glatch, Sean. "Irony Definition: Different Types of Irony in Literature." Writers.com, May 10, 2024. https://writers.com/irony-definition#irony-definition.

Got Questions. "What Does It Mean to Test God?" https://www.gotquestions.org/test-God.html.

———. "What Is the Significance of 40 Days in the Bible?" https://www.gotquestions.org/40-days-Bible.html.

Hamilton, James M., Jr. *Typology: Understanding the Bible's Promise-Shaped Patterns*. Grand Rapids: Zondervan, 2022.

———. "Was Joseph a Type of the Messiah? Tracing the Typological Identification Between Joseph, David, and Jesus." *Southern Baptist Journal of Theology* 12 (2008) 52–77.

"HaTikvah ('The Hope') Israel's National Anthem." The Goodman Camping Initiative for Modern Israel History, n.d. https://goodman.theicenter.org/sites/default/files/HaTikvah/index.pdf.

Heiser, Michael S. *The Unseen Realm: Recovering the Supernatural Worldview of the Bible*. Bellingham, WA: Lexham, 2015.

Helser, Jonathan, et al. "No Longer Slaves." *Peace*. Track 10. 2014.

Hundley, Michael. "What Is the Golden Calf?" *Catholic Biblical Quarterly* 79 (2017) 559–79.

Jackson, Peter, dir. *The Lord of the Rings: The Two Towers*. Burbank, CA: New Line Cinema, 2002.

"Lessons from Esther: A Female Perspective." In *Purim: God Saves His People*. 24–27. Chosen People Ministries, 2022. https://chosenpeople.com/lessons-from-esther-a-female-perspective/.

Levenson, Jon D. *Esther: A Commentary*. Louisville: Westminster John Knox, 1997.

Mackie, Tim. "God with Us (Matthew)." Tim Mackie Archives. YouTube video, 48:43. https://youtu.be/Y6XIeKYIEKI?t=865.

———. "What Prophecy Is For." *The BibleProject Podcast*, April 15, 2019. https://bibleproject.com/podcast/what-prophecy/.

Mark, Joshua J. "Egyptian Empire." World History Encyclopedia. https://www.worldhistory.org/Egyptian_Empire/.

Bibliography

———. "Hathor." World History Encyclopedia. https://www.worldhistory.org/Hathor/.

Merriam-Webster. "Syncretism." https://www.merriam-webster.com/dictionary/syncretism.

Midrash Tanchuma-Yelammedenu. Translated by Samuel A. Berman. Sefaria. https://www.sefaria.org/Midrash_Tanchuma%2C_Pekudei.2.3?lang=en.

Mitchell, David C. *The Message of the Psalter: An Eschatological Programme in the Book of Psalms*. Sheffield: Sheffield Academic, 1997.

One for Israel. "Jonathan Bernis: I Realized the Gospel Is Jewish!" https://www.oneforisrael.org/jewish-testimonies-i-met-messiah/jonathan-bernis-jewish-voice-testimony/.

"Parallels between Moses and Messiah." *The Chosen People* 29 (2023) https://www.chosenpeople.com/wp-content/uploads/2023/04/2304NL_APR7_Final.pdf.

Perrin, Norman. *The New Testament: An Introduction*. New York: Harcourt Brace Jovanovich, 1974.

Pill, Jeffrey. "In Search of . . . The Ten Commandments." YouTube video, 22:35. https://www.youtube.com/watch?v=upAqTn63INs.

Postell, Seth D. "Learning from Israeli Scholars How to Read the New Testament: An Example from Mark 4:35–41 1." *Academia* (2022). https://www.academia.edu/95511825/Learning_from_Israeli_Scholars_How_to_Read_the_New_Testament_An_Example_from_Mark_4_35_41_1.

———. "Reading Genesis, Seeing Moses: Narrative Analogies with Moses in the Book of Genesis." *Journal of the Evangelical Theological Society* 65 (2022) 437–55.

Postell, Seth D., et al. *Reading Moses, Seeing Jesus: How the Torah Fulfills Its Goal in Yeshua*. 2nd ed. One for Israel Ministry, 2017. Kindle ed.

Rydelnik, Michael, and Edwin Blum, eds. *The Moody Handbook of Messianic Prophecy: Studies and Expositions of the Messiah in the Old Testament*. Chicago: Moody, 2019.

Ryken, Leland. *How to Read the Bible as Literature*. Grand Rapids: Zondervan, 1984.

Sailhamer, John H. *The Pentateuch as Narrative: A Biblical-Theological Commentary*. Grand Rapids: Zondervan, 1992.

Schnittjer, Gary Edward, and Matthew S. Harmon. *How to Study the Bible's Use of the Bible: Seven Hermeneutical Choices for the Old and New Testaments*. Grand Rapids: Zondervan, 2024.

Sperber, A., ed. "Targum to Song of Songs." *The Bible in Aramaic*. 4 vols. Leiden: Brill, 1959–1968.

Tully, Eric. *Reading the Prophets as Christian Scripture*. Grand Rapids: Baker Academic, 2022.

"Who Are the Nephilim in Genesis 6?" Zondervan Academic, Apr. 12, 2018. https://zondervanacademic.com/blog/who-are-the-nephilim-in-genesis-6.

Wilder, James E., et al. *Joyful Journey: Listening to Immanuel*. East Peoria, IL: Shepherd's House, 2015.

Wilson, Marvin R. *Our Father Abraham: Jewish Roots of the Christian Faith*. Grand Rapids: Eerdmans, 1989. Kindle ed.

Zakovitch, Yair. "Through the Looking Glass: Reflections/Inversions of Genesis Stories in the Bible." *Biblical Interpretation* 1, 2 (1993) 139–52.

www.ingramcontent.com/pod-product-compliance
Lightning Source LLC
Chambersburg PA
CBHW072143160426
43197CB00012B/2229